Sleight of Mind

SUGGESTION AND MIND CONTROL
THE MENTALIST'S TOOLKIT

Copyright © 2004 Ian G Harling & Martin Nyrup

Published in Denmark by Spellbound,
www.spellbound.dk

Cover design by Morten Batting
Designed by Grand Danois a/s
www.danois.dk

2nd edition - 5th print - 2006

ISBN 87-990481-0-8

SLEIGHT OF MIND

Suggestion & Mind Control
The Mentalist´s Toolkit

Ian Harling & Martin Nyrup

Spellbound Publishing
Denmark

For my lovely wife, Helen

Ian Harling

For the love of my life, Janne

Martin Nyrup

With our deepest thanks to the many people too numerous to mention who have helped and inspired us during the creation of this book. Never again will you need to utter the words, "Will you just shut up about your bloody book for five minutes?!" We'll leave you alone now, honestly.

Preface

Mentalism requires a good understanding of how the human mind responds to the things it perceives, exploiting quirks of awareness and belief to create effects that can have a far deeper effect on your subjects and audiences than traditional magic. To this end, 'hypnotic' suggestion and NLP, the main focus of this book, are playing stronger roles than ever in modern mentalist performances. Unfortunately, finding accurate and useable information about either is much harder than it seems.

In light of this, we offer here a set of effects, tools and a range of techniques and sundry items taken from the core of NLP, hypnosis and well...other places far too numerous to mention. These skills can be put to use in many ways, not only to help you create your own routines, but also to give you an undoubted advantage over those around you in your daily life too. This might seem an extravagant claim, but learning about these things can and will change your view of human communication forever.

What we hope we've created here is the kind of book that both of us always wanted to discover hidden on a shelf somewhere. One of those books that you read and, every couple of pages, you smile cunningly to yourself and think, "I can use this..!" Objective but positive, this is a truthful look at subjects that until now have both enjoyed and suffered their own hyped-up reputations. No lies here about 'amazing hypnotic control', or the 'mind-reading and manipulation skills' of NLP, but a far more useful explanation of how you can use their real power to your advantage in any situation.

Please note however that we're not out to 'debunk' anyone. Although we aren't in complete agreement with everything that NLP or hypnosis proposes by any means, here we simply detail what we personally consider to be some of their most useful ideas. Every reader should of course go on to look at all the available evidence and make up their own minds about the nature of both NLP and hypnosis rather than taking our word - or anyone else's word for that matter - for what they entail.

We've also purposely avoided using too many of the terms commonly used by NLP to describe various aspects of their working systems, as we feel that readers with no previous experience of the latter may find some of them confusing. Those already familiar with NLP however will immediately realise for example that the 'Tactile' system we talk about is none other than the, 'Kinaesthetic' system. We make no apologies for replacing certain terms for less unwieldy words for the sake of clarity.

You'll notice that throughout this book we talk about things like performers and audiences, spectators and subjects and being 'on-stage'. But that isn't to say that we haughtily believe that only professional mentalists working to sizeable audiences would appreciate or even understand what's here. That's far from being the case, as it would be silly to angle a work like this at the small minority of magicians and mentalists who work professionally in the field. Please feel free to substitute 'workplace', 'party' or 'grandmother's house' for the words 'on-stage'; and the names of your long-suffering friends and family for 'spectators' and 'subjects'.

Whether you're looking for new ideas to base your routines on, or are simply interested in 'the good stuff' that you can use to baffle friends with, we're sure you'll find it here. Whoever you're performing for, we hope this will help you do it better.

Martin Nyrup & Ian Harling, December 2004.

Introduction

Is the world we each see around ourselves the same? Is what we as a whole perceive of reality representative of what's really 'here', wherever that may be?

Martin: "My niece is a lovely four year old girl who, for reasons beyond my grasp, thinks I'm the greatest magician to walk this Earth. She likes me to do simple magic, so a 'cups and balls' routine goes down particularly well with her, especially if the cups have bright colours. I do the trick, then she has even more fun playing with the cups on her own for the next hour or so. Easy, but gratifying audience.

"Recently, I decided to try something more interesting on her. So we sat down and cut a butterfly out of a piece of paper and then coloured it with crayons until she was happy with the result. I then placed it in the palm of my hand and knelt down before her and told her to watch it very carefully. After a few feeble movements the paper butterfly magically began to raise itself into the air and flutter around her. "Cups and balls?" I thought smugly, "Ha!"

"She watched its flight for a few moments as I congratulated myself on my magical abilities, but my smugness lasted all of about 30 seconds, whereupon my niece snatched the butterfly out of the air and shouted, "Now my turn!", then walked away. She never did comment on what I'd shown her.

"Now, you're probably thinking, "But what the Hell did you expect? The kid is four years old for God's sake!" But this was THE magic trick for the rest of my family, the solution to which was the one and only thing my 25 year old sister had on her Christmas wish list a few years back - and to this day still pesters me about. This was the same trick that, when I showed it to my girlfriend (replacing the butterfly with spoons that flew under her very nose one breakfast time), she threatened to withdraw certain marital rights unless I told her how it was done. It *always* got a good response. I was sure that my niece, age aside, would see it as a display of the grandness of my magic? But no.

"Later I realised that she wasn't impressed because in her world view what had happened was perfectly logical, not magical. So what if it was just a paper butterfly that we had coloured in together? For her butterflies fly, no big deal.

"I know that this example is a little extreme, as obviously a four year old will view things in a very different way than an adult, but it shows that we're only amazed by events that stretch our world-view, challenging what we believe to be possible. My niece and I simply have two different models of the same world. Where I have the benefit of experience - my niece has the far more appealing benefit of an as yet unspoiled imagination that's without the limitations and boundaries which inevitably come with advancing age."

Whereas most people are stunned by the skill of mentalists who seemingly (and in many cases it is only 'seemingly') read non-verbal cues in others, after a while even that becomes mundane. Too much exposure through TV and magazines to people who claim to do what were once extraordinary feats, such as muscle reading and spoon-bending, makes what they do gradually become almost the accepted norm. Whereas once these things stretched credulity to its limits, after our world view has been extended a few times, the amazing quickly becomes the mundane.

No matter who we are we each create our own model of the world, based on the impressions we receive through our five senses. But despite how much we think we see, feel and hear, only a very limited amount of the information we perceive ever finds its way into our conscious minds. The human race is simply not capable of accessing and processing the millions upon millions of impressions that bombard us daily. Author Tor Nørretrander comments in his excellent book, 'The User Illusion' that each of us receives approximately 11,000,000 pieces of information a second; whereas our conscious minds are only capable of making use of between 16 and 40 of them. To avoid becoming overwhelmed with sensory input we filter and prioritise information and build the world we believe is around us rather than see the one that's really there.

We all use three main filters to help process sensory input:

Omissions:

As stated above, our conscious minds aren't aware of everything that our subconscious mind is. To make matters worse we're generally appalling at remembering any information that *does* eventually find its way into our conscious minds. For instance, if you sat down and read this book for an hour and did your best to be aware of every word and idea within it, after just 24 hours at least 80 % of the detail will have been lost from your conscious mind and any hope of recall. Luckily most of the information loss can be prevented by the aid of various memory techniques; and some of the best are described by Tony Buzan in his wonderful 'Mind Set' series, which also contain some very excellent mnemonics and memory systems that any Mentalist can benefit from using.

Generalisations:

For the human mind to be able to process information more quickly we tend to generalise a very large chunk of what we receive and sum it up to create a holistic interpretation of events and data. There simply isn't time for us to actually address each and every piece of information given to us. When you see a car on the road you don't (usually) think, "Uh... There goes a red Ford Focus 2.0L Duratec 20." You simply think 'car'. If you meet someone new you don't consciously think, "45 year old male, balding, wrinkled, Caucasian member of the human race," you think 'person'.

Distortions:

Besides leaving out and generalising information we also tend to unknowingly distort it and regularly experience things other than how they really are. An example of this could be where an audience member swears that she saw a bluish glow surrounding your body during an effect, when in reality all you did was plant the *notion* of a glow appearing. In some cases you might even suggest *after your performance* that the glow had been there and have the subject 'remember' that this was the case. Our powers of recall are not only flawed, but easy to manipulate retrospectively. A few well-placed words can change beliefs and memories.

Having omitted, generalised and distorted so much information one would think that that should be enough to lose any kind of clear image of the 'real' world, but we don't stop there. We then take our impressions of the input that's gone through our mental filters and relate it to:

Our memories:

All our memories are stored as pictures, sounds, words, smells, tastes, body senses etc., and each memory may have the power to create an emotion or state of mind. But on the way into your long-term recall system memories can - and do - become very distorted and may lead to all kinds of emotional problems. If you've got a memory of a bad performance you've done for example, every time you think about it you may create a feeling of low self-worth in yourself. But was it really as bad as you remembered? It doesn't matter. Unless you work very hard to talk yourself out of this negative memory it might affect you so much that you decide never to perform again - without necessarily having a logical reason for you to base your decision on. And suddenly your bound for life by an event that may be only what you *think* has happened in the way it has.

Fundamental Structures:

Our fundamental structures are based on the vagaries of our character. Do we see the big picture all the time or just the small detail? Do we trust our own opinions or do we need to defer to somebody else's? Do we do things because we want to or because we feel we have to? Within NLP these structures are called 'Meta Programs', and are attempts to categorise our propensity to do one thing rather than another based on previous experiences and mental biases. We process input according to who we fundamentally are as human beings. If you're an introvert and we take the example from above of the bad performance, there's a good chance that it might make you want to lock yourself away at home. If you're outgoing by nature, the same experience might make you even more determined to make it work next time. Same input, two different outcomes.

Our convictions:

We create convictions about who we and others are, what we're capable of and what we believe reality to consist of. Convictions can be created through personal experiences, or inherited from our friends and family or foisted upon us by our culture or religion.

As you'll see as we continue, memories, structures and convictions can be altered by simple techniques that can cause some not quite so simple changes in perception. When not hampered by our conscious thoughts, the subconscious is capable of accessing, processing and storing information without us even realising it. Whereas you might not consciously notice the subtle crack of a rotten tree branch, your subconscious will note it and let your conscious mind know the second it thinks there's a danger of the branch falling on your head. In terms of pure, direct cognition (as we'll explain more of later) it's the subconscious that's in power. Control the subconscious through the use of suggestion or hypnosis and you control the conscious waking mind.

So why is all this of importance? Because of what's to follow. If you bear in mind the above information on why we choose (and the word choose is of real importance here) to behave as we do, everything we say subsequently will be that much easier to understand and utilise. Knowing for example that if you have two subjects, one of whom is a believer in telepathy or PK and the other who isn't, you have two different models of the world in front of you - and that you may choose to bias your performance towards either of them. If you were to do any routines with these participants that were seemingly based on telepathy then you'd obviously get two very different responses from each volunteer. Their beliefs may even make the difference between what you're doing working or not working at all. But once you begin to learn how simply we're swayed from even long-held beliefs, it becomes that much easier to create un-realities in the minds of your subjects whether they believe in what you're doing or not.

Before we begin to look closely at the many forms of suggestion and mental trickery that can be used as a basis for mentalism, let's first look at a way of making certain that the interaction between you and your subjects is all that it could be.

I

Rapport

Rapport; *Relationship. A pleasant feeling of mutual trust, affinity, and friendship established through verbal and non-verbal means.*

Rapport is the foundation on which every mentalist should build his or her performance, helping ensure that it has the best possible chance of success. It's where we should start - always, by creating a sense of co-operation and friendliness between the subjects we employ and ourselves. We don't need to become lifelong friends with anyone, we just need to make sure they're going to be happy, listen to (and act accurately upon) our instructions, and stay on 'our side' as we share the performance of the effect with them.

This isn't simply a quaint idea that we should learn how to 'get on' with our subjects just for the sake of it. In a little while you're going to be doing effects that operate directly on the subconscious mind that can only work if there is rapport between you and those people you use them upon.

Imagine you've chosen a participant to help you present your spectacular new mentalism routine and ended up with a drop-dead blonde girl - who absolutely hates you. How easy do you think it's going to be to bring her most intimate thoughts out in front of an expectant audience? To have her do exactly as you ask, to listen to what you have to say, to even care about the outcome of the trick?

Imagine instead ending up with a person that *you* find completely obnoxious and having to do a routine with him as the 'willing participant'. Without first establishing rapport he too will, if only on a subconscious level, feel your resistance towards him and therefore might not co-operate exactly as he should during the routine. Without co-operation, friendliness and a common desire to see the routine through to an auspicious end, how successful can it be?

But is it really possible to make a person like you who really doesn't, or to appear to like a person when *you* don't? In a word - 'yes'. And to be honest it's far easier than it sounds. The following two chapters will show exactly what techniques and subtleties can be used to create rapport between you and your subjects whenever you want to, allowing you to become a better and more likeable performer.

Having or not having rapport with the people we meet directly affects how successful we are, even how many opportunities are put our way. Few people give anything, let alone opportunities, to people they don't like.

We've all experienced 'good rapport' at some point in our lives. It's that feeling we get when we're talking to a person and everything outside the conversation doesn't matter. We're not constantly checking what we say before we speak, or worrying about how we look or how we stand. It's when we and the person we're talking to are relaxed and being ourselves. In this kind of atmosphere effects go more smoothly because you feel more confident; and the volunteer enjoys it more because it's a fuller, more exciting experience. You're sharing in enjoying the deceit with them, making them feel a part of what you're doing rather than them being just another prop.

Everything that follows in the next couple of chapters with regard to creating rapport and understanding the psychology of your subjects is based solely on a simple analysis of those you meet. Anyone can do it - and in fact many people already do without realising it.

The Systems

All of us have a favourite way of experiencing life, a 'primary sense', be that either visual, vocal, tactile or through internal dialogue. The way we talk, the way we move - everything about the way we behave demonstrates which of the four our favourite is. Look at the breakdown of each group below and try to work out which is your own preferred sense.

Visual People
- Think in pictures.
- Are very aware of colours, how things look, how one's self and others look.
- Body movements are often fast and will often be 'open' and directed upwards around head height.
- Breathing is often located high in the chest.
- Eye movements will tend to be upwards when images, ideas and comments are thought of.
- Visual people will often use words such as "see, recognise, draw, overlook, look, blind" etc.

Tactile People
- Think in terms of body sensations.
- Are very of aware of how things feel (i.e. how clothes feel against their bodies, does the light hurt their eyes, is the chair comfortable, etc.)
- Use very slow body movements and speak slowly.
- Gestures will be slow and around or below the stomach area.
- Breathing is often located in the lower part of the stomach.
- Eye movements tend to go to the lower right when emotions, ideas and comments are thought of.
- This system also includes your sense of taste and smell.
- Tactile people will often use words such as "go through, cold towards, run into, insensitive" etc.

Vocal People
- Think in sound.
- Are very aware of sounds and are easily distracted by them.
- Body language and pace of spoken language is found somewhere between 'visual' and 'feel'. Often display a 'listening' body.
- Gestures take place mainly over the middle part of the body.
- Breathing is often located in the diaphragm.
- Eye movements will go to the middle right or left when sounds, ideas and conversations are thought of.
- Vocal people will often use words such as "hear, recall, deaf, tell, unheard, speak" etc.

Internal People
- Think very logically.
- Like to use and be presented with ideas based on reason and system.
- Use slow body movements, often displaying the classic 'hand under the chin' listening position.
- Breath varies depending on which of the three above other systems they are most closely linked to.
- Eye movements will tend to go to the lower left when considering the internal dialogue of thoughts, ideas and comments.
- Internal people will often use words such as: inform, demonstrate, ignore, identify, remember, etc.

Of course, although you like everyone else use *primarily* one of these systems, that isn't to say that you can't be the type of person who uses more than one - or all of them as primary, secondary, tertiary, etc., systems - under the right conditions.

Being able to tell which systems your subject prefers - and changing your behaviour from your own system to theirs (displaying similar physical traits to them) will *always* establish good rapport between you and your subject. It's a part of our human psyche for us to warm to people who we believe are similar to us. Psychologists and counsellors have used similar methods of mimicry for years to establish trust between themselves and their clients. And all of us use less conscious methods of copycat behaviour each day in every conversation we take part in. If you're getting on with the person you're talking to you'll naturally mimic their body language without even thinking about it. They lean forward, you lean forward. They put their hand under their chin, or cross their arms and you do likewise. Even though it is largely subconscious behaviour, these signals are an intentional signal of friendliness, of being on the 'same wavelength' with the other person. It makes them think that you both feel the same way at the same time even if you're not actually talking. And obviously, if you think someone *does* feel the same way as you do then you'll come to like them far more quickly and deeply than you might have without that mirrored behaviour.

Everything we think is displayed somewhere on our faces or bodies. We're sure that at some time in the past you've had the feeling that a person is lying to you without you knowing why. I'm sure too that you've had the feeling that a person has said 'yes' to an invitation you've made, but you somehow knew they were not going to show. Some call this ability to know things without a sound factual reason, 'intuition', but perhaps in reality you're picking up on the constant subtle physical signals coming from another person and using them as a basis for this intuition? By learning to do this more consciously, as we show here, you can use this to your own advantage in countless ways.

These signals rule how we all interact with each other and actually create the person we are *perceived as* by each other.

2

The Analysis

The first real step in establishing rapport is to analyse your subject using the methods described below (and a few more that we'll explain shortly) to find out what kind of a person they are and what they'll respond best to. You then adjust your behaviour so that it closely matches the subject's own, fine-tuning it until you've fully established rapport. To do all this you must understand the subject's state of mind, which you can do by simply observing changes in their non-verbal behaviour.

Doing this 'analysis' is really nothing more than listening to and looking at the person in front of you; and, if need be, occasionally asking non-threatening and open questions to obtain or verify further output. But - and tattoo these words in big letters on the forehead of a close loved one as a permanent reminder - BE SUBTLE!! It can be easy to seem creepy and a little bit weird when you're questioning people and copying them like this. Too long a look in someone's eyes at the wrong moment will make them suspect that you're up to something, even if they don't know what. Be natural, be observant, be clever - but watch what you give away too, the other person might be as naturally adept at reading your signals as you are theirs.

Note too that we are *not* suggesting that anyone simply copy another person's behaviour outright. That would also be so unnatural (unless in a moment of deep rapport) that it would again trigger warnings in your subject's mind. You will, if you persist in wildly copying or noticeably and continually observing another's behaviour without apparent good reason, end up eating mushy food with your fingers in a home where the windows have bars. Do not do it.

Mimic in small ways, begin slowly. Every now and again you can test for depth of rapport by changing your own body to a new position and seeing if they copy *you* in any way. In a good natural conversation where people are getting on, they tend to take turns at moving to a new body position. As the conversation deepens their behaviour will grow more mirrored. If they're lovers however, their mirroring can become total, mentally and physically.

Try this. It's a strange example of what deep mirroring feels like, what kind of feelings it triggers in us all. You're going to have to do this physically, not just imagine it - and with full conviction. Maybe after a drink or two. Maybe nobody watching either, okay? Remember the mushy food and the bars? At home, curtains closed.

Imagine that you are laid on a bed - bear with us here! - with a member of the opposite sex. Clothed even. You lay facing each other. Close. You look into each other's eyes for a few seconds then kiss, softly, briefly. Closing your eyes you lean your head forward until it gently touches his/hers in exactly the same place. You both move slowly, a gentle rolling of your heads where they touch, in perfect unison. Your eyes stay closed as you enfold the other person in your arms, their arms wrapping around you likewise in perfect symmetry. Your neck and the side of your face is against theirs, you roll your necks and heads together, almost like swans, your movements perfectly mimicking each other. Your cheeks touch then roll away to foreheads, then noses, then lips, chins and necks, backs of heads, over and over in slow random whorls and give up to the feelings that ensue...

Now, you might say that just thinking about doing that even without the other person mimicking you would obviously encourage a 'pleasant' response. It would be a nice position to be in, obviously. But if the other person is moving exactly as you are, then what you begin to feel is far deeper. Not only does mirroring at this level imply complete rapport, even love, from and for the other person, it creates within us emotions and feelings that are very hard to describe. The kiss at the beginning of the above is a very useful method of getting people to focus very acutely on the moment, helping them experience the sensations this mirroring creates much more deeply. Pity this mechanism can't be used more often in our performances..!☺

Subconsciously everyone analyses the behaviour of those they meet, looking for, amongst other things, examples of mirroring. We want to be wanted, and we always look out for signs that may indicate that we are whether we realise it or not. Whereas in most people this analysis is subconscious, it must be obvious how it would pay to have it under your conscious control instead. The hard part is of course knowing what to listen and look for, so let's go through some aspects of that first.

Our meaning of the word 'analysis' here will be the process of you understanding the non-verbal signs that other people display. This is something you need to work on to become good at, but luckily it's not very difficult once you understand the basic concepts behind it. Your opportunities to practise this skill are of course around you every single day, during simple conversations. When you're talking to people, try being more aware of the things we suggest below and you'll quickly begin to know things about their thoughts you wouldn't think were possible. With practise this process of analysis will become second nature to you and will give you endless information about those you meet. Although we give a basic synopsis of the main things to look out for here, take a look at the later chapter, 'More Signals' to help you take this much further.

So, when talking with anyone you want to analyse you're looking for non-verbal signs and physiological changes that include:

Openness of the eyes

How open or closed are the other person's eyes? This will tell you a lot about how the person feels towards what's being communicated. For instance, very open eyes show attentiveness, surprise and so forth. Slightly closed or squinting eyes demonstrates mistrust, disagreement, etc.

Eye focus and pupil size

Where your subject's eyes focus tells you whether you have their attention - and rapport - or not. Also, do the eyelids flicker - and if they do, why? Is it nervousness, low self-esteem, are they uncomfortable with you or the things that you or they are saying?

Pupil diameter can be difficult to estimate as you wont have a mean size to refer to, but it can still be useful to look for any major changes. Use it as an indication of whether or not you're making correct 'hits' with your statements about the subject. If a person gets excited or nervous because of something you've said or done the pupils will visibly grow.

Position of the head
Demonstrates attentiveness/thoughtfulness. Can also tell you a great deal about whether the person has a preference for the vocal system, as people who prefer this system will often tilt their head's slightly when being attentive.

Colour of the skin
Is it red, pale, light, dark, shining or dull?

Muscles of the face
Are they tight or relaxed?

Breathing
Fast or slow breathing tells you if the person is relaxed or nervous. Where is their breathing located? Is it in the stomach, diaphragm or breast? The lower it is the more relaxed the subject feels.

Hands
Open/closed/fumbling? Relaxed, nervous etc.

Changes in symmetry and balance of face and body
An 'uneven' face or body tends to show that the subject disagrees with you.

Pitch of voice
High, low, monotonous or varied. All indicators of which systems are in play and whether the person is relaxed, nervous, highly strung, bored, indifferent etc.

Speed of speech

Fast/slow. Again good indicators of the persons general state of mind.

Fullness of the voice

Fullness and volume tend to show confidence growing or decreasing.

As your ability grows you'll discover lots of other things to look/listen/feel for which you can add to your ever-expanding range of 'things to analyse', thus enhancing your ability to cold read any subject. But the eyes have another means of conveying information that we're going to look at now, an obvious but largely overlooked area of analysis.

The eyes have it...

By simply watching people's eye movements you may be able to tell whether they're thinking in pictures, sounds or words; whether they're creating what they're saying or remembering it. We all have a series of 'places' that we look at, both physically and mentally, to retrieve information. We look at a place with our eyes to access a place in our minds. As we lie about something for the first time the majority of people will, for example, move their eyes to look up and to the right to formulate a visual scene. Although there are of course exceptions - and you would do a further test to verify any deductions you make using this method - the eye positions that the following list details are those that people *most commonly* use when performing mental tasks .

Visual
- When we mentally construct pictures, we look up and to the right.
- When we remember pictures we look up and to the left.

Aural
- When we construct sounds or words we look to the middle right.
- When we remember sounds or words we look to the middle left.

Tactile
- When we think about what we're physically feeling we look down and to the right.

Internal
- When we are having an internal dialogue, we look down and to the left.

There are of course no 100% perfect systems, so use this chart as a beginning, helping you establish what the subject's actual system is. This illustration should make the system of eye movements much easier to understand. Note that this is how the other person looks, a mirror image of what you yourself actually do.

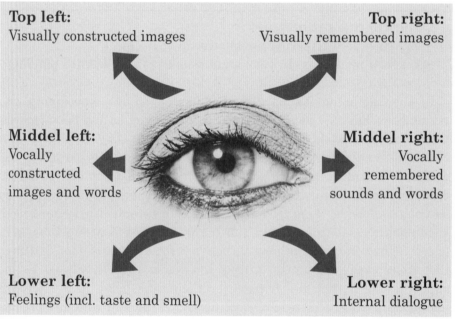

Top left:
Visually constructed images

Top right:
Visually remembered images

Middel left:
Vocally
constructed
images and words

Middel right:
Vocally
remembered
sounds and words

Lower left:
Feelings (incl. taste and smell)

Lower right:
Internal dialogue

Figure 1 - Standard Eye Movements

There's a range of questions you might ask to force your subject's eye movements:

Remembered visual image, ask:
- What's the colour of the card you chose?
- Remember which hand I hid the coin in?

Constructed visual image, ask:
- If you could decide, which colour card would you want?
- Now imagine the glass of water turning red...

Remembered sounds, ask:
- What call tune do you currently have on your mobile?
- Remember the last song you heard played on the radio.

Constructed sounds, ask:
- Imagine me whispering the answer in your ear.
- I have a music box. In your mind decide on a melody it's playing.

In the beginning it's hard to keep track of eye movements *and* remember what they mean - but with a bit of practise and perseverance this technique can do wonders.

Watch the directions people look in as they speak to see if you can recognise which pattern they use. Once you get used to doing this it's *relatively* easy to tell when someone is telling the truth or not, as long as you're allowing them to act naturally. To establish whether or not your subject uses this system you could simply ask where they were from and how long they'd lived there. They'll try to remember and go to the upper right, instantly letting you know that they'll go to the opposite side if they lie. If however their eyes move to the top left instead you know that you're dealing with a person who mirrors the system. And, having established that, you can continue by simply reversing the labels on the eye positions shown above. We have to say that it's not very often that you'll encounter a 'mirrorer' but it does happen, so it's always a good idea to do a quick check like this to be sure. Note that this is a test, not part of an effect. Don't base a routine on making your initial analysis, hoping that the chart above will apply to your current subject.

Although this is an excellent tool it does have some drawbacks. A good liar commits more and more details of his lie to memory on each subsequent telling of it. Once it's firm in his mind he'll look up and to the left to retrieve it instead of to the right to create it, making an older lie harder to spot. Be well aware too that your subject isn't honour bound to answer even your test question truthfully either, and could leave you unknowingly without a control to base any deductions about his eye system on.

We're sure you can understand how, when handled correctly, this can be very powerful in the hands of any mentalist, allowing him or her to gain very useful information from the subject without them ever knowing that you've done so. Imagine the possibilities this holds for cold reading and 'telepathic' effects...

Just a few tips on general usage:

- Don't explain what you're doing to your subjects or even give a hint of it when you're trying out the above. If you do you're likely to find that they'll try to control their eye movements, thus rendering all of this useless. If you were to say to somebody, "Give me a list of five objects you have at home - but lie about one of them", your wording and the very fact that you've asked them at all would suggest that you're going to try to guess which is the fictitious object. Faced with this direct challenge many people will do their best to hide any natural movements of their eyes as they give you the list. Whether they answer and allow their natural eye movements to take place or not rests, to a high degree, on how you've phrased your initial question. However, if you can catch people on the hop they'll usually be more natural than if they've been given any warning, so hurrying them into a response will help. Although this technique can and does work well on those subjects who are open and co-operative, you can never guarantee that it will work on everyone. Many people really are excellent liars and neither this nor anything else is foolproof against them.

- Don't ask someone to compile a list of objects in their minds too long before you're to 'guess' which it is. Obviously, once an imaginary object is on a memorised list with real objects, the subject will not go to one side to *create* the imagined object as they should. However, there should still be clues that will give away the lie. Look out for a quick flick away from your gaze, or any of the non-verbal cues we mention later that might indicate stress in the subject.

- The speed at which the eyes move and how much time they stay in each position varies greatly from person to person. Practise and experience are paramount if you're going to track these movements and be able to 'read' people accurately.

- Some people experience pictures, sound, feelings and internal dialogue by looking straight ahead. Needless to say the technique does not work on them. They are luckily very far and few between though!

If you *should* one day run into one of these people we have an additional neurological feature that you can use that will work on anyone:

Place say, three objects on a table in front of a subject. Tell them to lift each item up in front of their eyes, look at it for a few seconds and then put it down again. Once they've done this with all the objects, ask them to choose just one item without telling you which. Now get the person to focus their eyes on the table and keep them there. You place each item in their view one at a time and let the subject look at them for a few seconds. Having gone through all of the items you are then able to tell which they chose. How?

As they look at the items one at a time you watch the pupils of their eyes very carefully. When the mentally chosen item comes into view their pupils will dilate. Although they might try to trick you, their eyes won't lie. Watch out for sudden pupil dilation in other situations too, it's a handy indicator of sudden emotional stress, positive or negative.

3

The Match

Of course, creating rapport isn't just a case of learning to interpret the signals that other people 'project', we also need to learn to match the signals *we* put out to the taste of whoever we're trying to establish rapport with. By subtly matching the visual, vocal and tactile input we get from people, we can easily establish rapport with them.

As with the 'analysis' process we mentioned earlier, this matching (and mismatching too) is something that you've always done, perfectly naturally, every day of your life. And still there's a good chance that you've never consciously been aware of it or the amazingly influential power it has over us all.

Next time you go anywhere where there are a lot of people gathered, try and watch how they're all communicating with each other. If you look closely you'll notice how those who have naturally good rapport are mirroring each other's body movements. Listen closely and you'll notice too that they seem to use many of the same words, speak in the same tone of voice and may even breath in the same rhythm. Important and as obvious as this is, most of it will be completely lost on those actually having the conversation. They just send and receive signals subconsciously, not really knowing why they feel the way they do about the person in front of them.

Of course, if you're looking at people who are obviously not in agreement what you'll see and hear will, after reading the above, be quite obviously mismatched body language. No shared words or phrases, no mimicry of signals - there will be no rapport between these people at all.

Find a subject you've never met before and try the following as you engage them in conversation. It can be difficult at first to concentrate on both having a conversation and watching how the person is responding, but persevere.

Start off carefully. Sit as they do without overdoing it. 'Subtle' is the keyword here, always subtle. If you're too obvious at this stage then the other person might think you're making fun of them, or being obviously manipulative, and you'll end up with a mismatch. Note too that you don't have to match a complete gesture - such as your subject's crossed arms - and can instead use what NLP calls 'representational matching', where you would instead grip your wrist or hold one arm diagonally across your chest to give the subtle impression of a match. If they lean back in their chair with their fingers locked behind their heads, you could just lean back with one of your arms resting on the chairs side. This is just as effective as direct mimicry and much less easy to detect.

Watch how (rhythm, speed, position) they move their hands and match it. If the person tends to make large movements around head height, bring up your hands to match theirs, but do it on a smaller scale, thus making your matching less obvious. Now look at how the person is breathing and try discreetly to match this too. This is an extremely powerful matching tool and almost nobody will consciously notice you're doing it. Unconsciously though they will love it!

Listen to the tone of their voice and slowly begin to mesh with it and their style of speech. Again this mustn't be too obvious so don't go from what might be your normal, high-pitched voice to a low-pitched speaking voice in a matter of a few seconds. Gradually. Listen too to the words they use and the way they build sentences. Use words they favour or those that are similar. If they like to use slang then speak slang. If they speak in metaphors then make sure to throw in your own when it's convenient. Learn to delay this matching so that it'll become less obvious what you're doing. Watch and listen constantly for all the various signals described in the analysis, they'll give you valuable information about how well your efforts to create rapport are going.

Matching body language, voice and words has a profound effect, so look out for:

Body language:
Gestures
Body posture
Mimicry (the subject's mimicry of you)

Voice:
Volume
Tone
Rhythm
Fullness of voice

Words:
Regularly use of particular words or phrases
Dialect
Slang
Metaphors
Phrasing/rhythm

To mismatch is not necessarily a bad thing and it's a tool well worth learning. You might be put in a situation where you need to end the rapport you've established, which would be done simply by mismatching whatever signals you're receiving. If someone were speaking slowly and deeply you'd speak quickly and in a higher register. If they were sitting down and resting their hands quietly on their knees then you would stand up and gesticulate excessively. You might let your eyes flicker to something more interesting in the room as they speak, or more extremely, simply to turn your back on them. It really is that simple.

If you're performing in the street or in a restaurant it's very hard to pick and choose exactly who's gong to take part in any effect. Even with years of experience you can be thrust unwittingly into a situation where you simply *have* to use whoever's at hand, which can sometimes be disastrous. If this should happen to you try to mismatch. It can be unnerving in a subtle psychological way for all but the most single-minded subjects and you should find that this person will quickly back down. You don't need to mismatch much to make this work, as soon as you start to mismatch most people will understand instinctively that it's time to move away.

As with everything in this book, practise and experience are paramount, so give as much time as you can to learning and understanding these techniques. Embrace failure when you practise, it will make you wiser next time around and help you avoid making the same mistakes twice.

Putting It All Into Practise

You can push your subjects towards a positive mood very easily by giving them positive signals that they will, if you have rapport, mimic. We call this 'to guide' or to 'lead' the subject - although once you're adept at creating rapport you may not need to go as far as using the following to lead the participant.

You have a volunteer who is very nervous about suddenly being the centre of attention. He speaks rapidly, his eyes flicker, he begins to sweat, etc. You begin by making him believe that you're on the same wavelength as he is. You match his pace of breathing, speaking at the same rapid pace and in the same tone that he does, subtly copying his body movements, etc. *without making it obvious that this is what you are doing*!!! You seem to share his anxiety, gaining his confidence really through nothing more than seeming to share a common mental state.

With rapport established you now guide the subject into a calmer state of mind. Slowly - but never obviously - changing the pace of your breathing, slowing it down. Slowing the pace and deepening the tone of your voice. Shoulders down. Keep your hands relaxed and move them slowly, holding them down around your stomach or thighs but never in between. This helps you seem less defensive and therefore by inference, happy with your subject's presence. He wants to be liked too, so he'll be pleased to see this behaviour in you. Also, use palm-up gestures - though don't overdo it - with your hands spread apart from your body to help you seem more open and genuine.

What will quickly happen is that your volunteer will follow your changes in behaviour and start to relax too. He does this because you've established rapport and he's in 'sync' with you. He likes you because you seem to like him. Humans are easy touches. We're weak☺ Subconsciously he'll now follow your guidance and let you take him down to a calmer and more relaxed state of mind.

If you do this properly he won't even notice what you've done. It might sound as if it takes a long time to accomplish this kind of effect, but it can actually be done in a matter of minutes once you know how. But, we don't mean to imply by this or anything above that your efforts to gain rapport are isolated from the rest of your routine and confined solely to its commencement. Rapport building and re-building is done constantly throughout your contact with any subject or subjects. In essence, rapport isn't some lock down state from which your subject wont emerge until you send him or her on their way. It's a state of trust, a relationship that's just as prone to destruction as any other sort of relationship is. A simple, but misplaced gesture or facial expression - or just hurrying them along towards relaxation too quickly - can ruin it entirely.

Exercise:

Stop reading for an hour or two and take a trip into the 'real' world. Find a bench, sit down and watch people. At some point a person is bound to sit beside or in front of you. Without being obvious, observe the person and try to establish rapport with them without speaking to them. Mirror the person in subtle ways. If you feel rapport has been established, slowly try to guide the person to a different body posture. Move your legs to another position and you'll find that they will follow. Move body posture and the person will follow.

You might find that the person will then talk to you, simply because of this subtle rapport. If they continue to try to establish verbal rapport before you've completed your guidance process they may already be feeling that they actually know and like you.

Summary

Let's just briefly look at what you've achieved so far. By now you should have a pretty good understanding by now of all the basic things you need do and appreciate to help you establish good rapport:

- The most common systems of behaviour
- How to read eye movements
- How to analyse verbal and non-verbal signals
- Matching and mismatching

Try to see all this as just different aspects of a single tool, designed to help you establish strong rapport as quickly as possible. You can, to some extent at least, get away with some pretty awful performance mistakes once you've established rapport with someone. They see what you want them to see, do what you want them to do, because they're happy to do so. They become almost literally blind to the world (and your errors), wanting the effect to work as much as you do; whereas a person with whom you've not established rapport will spot the dodgy looking 'Swami' writer hanging from your thumb pretty quickly. It can't not help to be able to get people to feel liked and wanted as they assist you with a routine. It really is that simple.

Many people insist that all of this is a complicated science that takes years of study, but sorry, it's not. Learn and practise what you've read here and you'll quickly gain a valuable tool that can work wonders - in every aspect of your life.

4

More Signals

We're now going to look at non-verbal cues in more detail to give you a much better chance of knowing how your subjects are feeling about what's happening to them as you perform. Obviously it'll pay to try to commit as many of the following to memory as possible. For those of you who see, as we do, the whole business of non-verbal cues as being an incredibly powerful tool, it will be useful if you also go on to explore the work of people like psychologist Paul Ekman on 'micro-expressions'. Although much more subtle than the very visual gestures here, micro-expressions are very hard to fake and are far more telling. Sometimes as brief as one-one-hundred-twenty-fifth of a second, these non-verbal cues are too fast for most people to recognise on a conscious level, but after just a little training, even novices can learn to decode them consciously. For more details see: www.paulekman.com

Lying

In a way we mentalists are professional liars - and if we are going to lie then it's in our own best interest to tell those lies exceptionally well. If we say all the right things with our bodies we're adding a second level of conviction to any deceit we're trying to perpetrate with our voices. If we can also read *another's* body language then we can discover how much the other person is believing in what we say.

Poker players, themselves ardent students of body language, usually say that a player who's bluffing will tend to suppress most natural body movements (such as head nodding, hand gestures, etc) in an attempt to hide ALL signals from observers to conceal the lie. People who are telling the truth on the other hand will tend to be over-animated, attempting to show that the normal non-verbal cues that would give away their lies are not present.

Apart from the eye movements, increased pupil dilation and body language we've already talked about, there are a lot of other cues listed below that *might* show when the subject isn't telling the truth. Hiding the mouth (or corner of the mouth) for example is a good indicator of lying, but also of scepticism - and unfortunately indigestion too.☺ This is far from being an exact science, as a good liar is aware of all his give-away cues and can repress all but the most deeply ingrained of them. Note too that as Ekman has said, "'the fear of being disbelieved looks the same as the fear of being caught lying...'"

However we don't want to fall into the trap of over-playing the importance of non-verbal communication to the detriment of other means of interaction. Non-verbal and direct verbal suggestions and cues are equally important. But some branches of therapy and NLP still rely heavily on the 'fact' that we humans supposedly communicate only 7% of information by the actual words we use, with 55% communicated by body language and 38% by the pitch and tone of our voices. In actuality this ratio is badly skewed because of a misinterpretation of the data and experiment it was based upon.*

The originator of this ratio, Albert Mehrabrian Ph., detailed it in his two books, 'Silent Messages' (1971) and 'Non-verbal Communications' (1972). In 'Silent Messages' he shows that the ratio only concerns what he calls the, '...resolution of inconsistent messages...' - in NLP terminology, 'incongruencies' - and that very few things can be communicated non-verbally. In an informal interview in 1994 with 'Buzz' Johnson, Mehrabrian said that his data and inferences were not meant to be applied to normal communications and were of very limited application.

For more information about this misunderstanding,
go to the online article, 'The Myth of Non-Verbal Dominance', at
http://www.borg.com/~rparkany/CDA/NonverbalDominanceMyth.html
-originally published in 'Anchor Point', July 1994), by Dr. C. E. "Buzz"
Johnson. Johnson is a respected NLP practitioner who has, 'gone
through both NLP 'Master Practitioner' and 'Trainer's Training' and
now researches the power of words in a variety of different disciplines,
medicine, education, addictions, relationships, psycho-neuro-
immunology hypnosis, psychotherapy, , etc.'

We wont describe the experiment that gave rise to these figures here, though it makes interesting reading to see how they've been perpetuated and never questioned over the years. But it doesn't really matter to us as performers whether words convey 7% of information or 70%, because in truth things like body language and vocal qualities form a subtle means of communication all of their own that can have all the complexities and impact of a spoken language. If you understand how to read these signals well in others, (and we don't really want to overplay the reality of this here, but...) everything changes. You learn how not to frighten off potential friends or lovers, to seem confident, to understand when someone objects to something you've said or wants more proof of it, when someone wants to buy into what you're saying or instead just walk away. If you can't 'speak' body language (and most of us can't consciously) then every day can be a series of missed opportunities.

The Signals

Whereas at one time it was thought that our body language was culture-specific, newer research has shown that not only are these signals universal, but are hard-wired physical reactions to specific emotions. We can't avoid reacting as we do when certain ideas and emotions arise, it just happens too quickly for us to stop unless we're very aware and capable. As this is the case, some of these signals (such as 'Hand to Back of Head') are infallible.

Be aware that some of these 'Tells' (non-verbal cues in Poker parlance) do have multiple meanings and that children use many of them in different ways than adults, though the emotions they indicate in any particular case should be fairly evident from the context that they're being used in.

If you're ever unsure of why someone is projecting the signals they are, mentally (or preferably physically) act them out and see how they make you yourself feel. In terms of the signals that you personally want to give out, think about how you can use the first three here to help your performance.

Of course many of these signals are not used alone, but in conjunction with other signals (for example, Palm Down and Shoulder Alignment) to give even stronger messages.

Steepled Fingers. Fingers in a 'steeple' position whilst talking, listening or thinking are used to convey an idea that the user is in deep reflection. Of course, it's also used by people who want to at least *appear* to be thinking deeply about something too. "I am listening/speaking /thinking and considering what you/I say very carefully."

Parallel Palms. The palms of the speaker's open hands are held facing each other and usually used together in a chopping motion to emphasise particular words or ideas or to show personal conviction in the truth of what's being said. "This is what I believe to be the case and what I think we should do about it..."

Palms Face Down. Another movement used to emphasise the 'truth' of words or phrases or the authority of the speaker. Tends to be used to say, "I mean this..." or, "What you've just said is all well and good, but...." or, "Hold on, let's calm down." When used with strong downward beating movements it makes what we say seem more convincing. As a general signal it has a tendency to seem unfriendly or argumentative if used too much.

Palm Up. As we don't naturally use palm up gestures, they're one of the few signals that we use consciously. Usually used to signal submission, almost handing one's fate over to another, it shows helplessness and uncertainty, especially when used in conjunction with a shoulder shrug.

Adam's-Apple Jump. This looks very much like gulping or swallowing. It shows stress and anxiety or a disagreement with what has just been said.

Angular Distance (of shoulder position towards or away from the subject). Angular distance provides us with a pretty much infallible means of judging how we feel about those around us. We can't help but square our shoulders towards those we like and agree with and away from those we don't.

Squaring your shoulders towards another person is usually an invitation for them to speak. Holding a conversation with someone with your upper body angled away from them can clearly signal that you may not be interested in them, or are feeling unfriendly towards them, or may even fear them.

If someone is hoping to bring a conversation to an end (even if they like the person they're talking to) they'll tend to show their intent to leave with their shoulders, face and/or feet, turning them away in the direction they intend to move off in (this is a 'Cut-off' signal).

When in groups, some people will talk with a number of other members of the gathering, freely moving their heads and eyes in various directions - but will all the while remain with their upper body pointing towards the dominant or most liked member of the group.

Gaze Avoidance. Gaze avoidance is so deeply 'wired-in' to our reactions that it can be an excellent Tell. It can denote scepticism (usually used with a sudden look upwards and to one side), invasion of personal space, or guilt.

Gaze down. Eyes looking downwards rather than to the side shows guilt or submission. Looking into another's eyes can increase anxiety and give the sense that the other person may be able to see our true emotions - whilst breaking eye contact lowers our stress levels. People who feel, or want to appear, to be dominant will hold eye contact much longer with those they feel to be subordinate to them. However, remember that the reason the other person might not be able to maintain eye contact with you could be simply that they like you!

Arms crossed. Although many people equate this with anxious, defensive postures, in fact it can also mean, "I'm happy and comfortable," or a haughty, "This had better be good...". The difference between the two can best be decided by looking at how tightly the arms are crossed and how closely the elbows are held into the body of the subject. The tighter they are the more defensive the person is feeling. How 'big' the crossed arms are made to appear can reflect how disdainful the subject is of you.

Chin Jut. Tilting your head back and pointing your chin towards another shows a subtle intent to attack or a disliking for those your engaging with. An extension of this, ('Rearing') rising up and leaning slightly backwards, usually means arrogance, disbelief and disliking for. "Oh yeah? You and who's army...?"

Blinking. A 'normal' blink rate in humans is around 20 a minute, with anything more than this usually indicating shyness, fear or guilt.

Flexion Withdrawal. Pulling the hands away from a speaker (especially noticeable if you're seated at a table) tends to show dislike and even fear, removing the limb from apparent or potential harm.

Arm Reach. Again, most visible when people are sitting across a table from each other, indicating a subconscious desire to touch the other person or to increase the depth of rapport with them.

Hand Behind Head. Holding/touching the back of the neck with an open palm shows uncertainty, negativity, conflict or possibly being discovered in a lie. Can also be used to show that the speaker wants to appear uncertain and less aggressive about something he is saying to reduce its impact. Lesser versions of this signal are touching the side of the neck, scratching or tugging at an ear lobe or touching the cheek. The amount of 'guilt' or stress being felt is usually proportionate to the amount of force being applied by the hand to the neck and the length of time it stays in this raised position.

Head Tilt (towards the left or right shoulder). When used with a slight raising of the shoulder, may indicate friendliness and help create rapport. Also used to show coyness, submission or deference. Without the shoulder raise it can indicate incredulity.

Feet Pointing. Someone who disagrees with what you're saying will tend to have their feet pointing away from you, showing their desire to walk away or escape from you.

Lip Compression. Pursing the lips has a number of uses, signalling dislike, anger, sadness, uncertainty or disagreement. It's also commonly used when someone is thinking hard about an awkward task they're doing.

Lip Touch (with fingers or an object). Can indicate such a range of emotions that it can be hard to get a definitive meaning unless used with other signals. It may indicate stress, fear or uncertainty - or even sudden thoughtfulness. However, it's closely linked to thumb-sucking as a source of comfort, so will usually signify that the speaker is under stress or anxious. If you're speaking to someone who Lip Touches as you say something, they may be indicating that they have an unexpressed opinion or idea about what you've just said, using the movement as a way of visually indicating that this is the point where they would like to interject.

Self-Touching. The more stressed we become the more we unconsciously touch our bodies to gain comfort. Scratching, pinching and rubbing at the skin (at the wrists for example) can also show lying, dislike, fear, disagreement, or uncertainty. Obviously, as this is the case it's best to avoid this kind of movement when trying to create rapport.

Shoulder Shrug. Indicates uncertainty, submissiveness or resignation - and will usually be used by a speaker to non-verbally contradict a statement of assent. For example, giving a shoulder shrug when saying something like, "Okay, I'll do it", tends to indicate that the speaker has no desire to do whatever is being asked of them and will therefore probably do it badly.

Tongue Show. When the subject's tongue pokes out briefly from between their lips it will usually signify uncertainty, disliking or displeasure and will tend to show *contradiction* to any statements the speaker has made, such as, "I'm happy with that," or "I agree."

Nose Touch. Touching the side of the nose with a finger is a strong sign of uncertainty.

Pitch of Voice. As well as showing levels of stress in your subjects, the pitch of the voice is also a useful way of telling who is dominant and who is subservient in any exchange. If a subject interjects comments in a higher pitch than the person who is speaking, the more they're trying to show subservience and/or interest in what the other person is saying. Men may also tend to speak in a much higher pitch when in a female dominated group to try to show non-aggression and ingratiate themselves into the group.

5

Anchors

Anchors are cues associated with particular emotions, which are in turn linked to specific memories. Think of them as being triggers that release the emotional content that memories carry. You might for example associate certain songs with events in your life - both happy and sad - and find that simply hearing the first bars of these tunes will bring back all kinds of vivid emotional associations. Tastes and smells in particular can trigger incredibly deep and detailed memories going right back to early childhood, causing you to recall not just a vague event, but sometimes the entire emotional content of your mind at that point. You remember what it was like to be you at this particular moment in your life, almost in totality.

Memories and anchors are so closely entwined that it's very hard to see where one stops and the other begins. If you'd like to trigger a recoil response in a volunteer then you might begin by creating an atmosphere of tension and foreboding and, at a critical moment nod your head sharply as you pull on a hidden thread that passes through the subject's hair. If you repeat this a couple of times the sensations they feel will become anchored to the movement of your head and you may then be able to trigger a recoil by simply making that gesture without the use of the thread. The subject subconsciously associates a particular movement with a disagreeable outcome and responds accordingly. Even though it may seem impossible to them that you could create this effect with a simple nod of your head, they wont be able to over-ride the fact that experience has just taught them that this movement signals a physical effect upon their hair that they will react to, regardless of whether they can feel something or not.

Creating anchors in ourselves is perfectly natural and we use them all the time to help us remember potentially damaging/gratifying actions and events. We touch a hot kettle as children and forever associate the pain of the burn we receive with that touch, reminding us not to do it again in future without being aware of the consequences. Whether we call this process 'anchoring', 'suggestion' or simply 'remembering' is a moot point, but there's no doubting its effectiveness.

Anchors are everywhere - and in such a large quantity that we hardly notice them. Marketing people thrive on anchors and (ab)use them severely to generate emotional responses to their products. Images of babies and kittens are used in advertising to create in the viewer a direct association between the product and feelings of love and warmth. On a more simplistic level, images of thirsty people in sweltering heat are used to trigger a desire to drink. Even seeing a green traffic light on the road side in an advertisement can cause a relaxation response in some drivers.

One thing that marketing companies and we mentalists have in common is that we both seek to control the emotional state of our 'clients'. And this is basically what an anchor does, helping you trigger particular emotions which you can then take and use to create a specific frame of mind or sensation in your subjects - or even make them choose a particular card or object over another. If for example you were to offer five cards to a participant, their natural propensity would be to take the card at position 4 if they were to just pick one without thinking about it. But if you were to anchor a gesture, sound or image to one particular card you could in many cases steer them away from this tendency and free choice. In his excellent book, 'Psychological Subtleties', Steve Banachek asks a volunteer to choose a number between 17 and 21, then recites each number in the same voice until he gets to the required force, whereupon he softens his tone to create a subtle subliminal anchor. Simple as this is it's enough to cause a high percentage of subjects to pick the desired card. Note that although you could alternatively anchor the required card to a firmer vocal delivery, your subject and audience may tend to recognise this immediately as a direct attempt at influencing the choice the subject makes, so it's best to use cues that 'negatively' stress the force object, as they're less obvious. Giving suggestion in this way is something that can only be learned through experience and practise.

In 'Pure Effect', Derren Brown suggests a variety of excellent uses for anchors, including anchoring the subject's sense of wonder at the culmination of an effect, which he then might choose to trigger at the end of a second effect to create an even bigger response in the subject.

Our minds store a vast range of memories of events and information that we've gleaned throughout our lives, many of them carrying strong emotional content. If we can get a subject to recall such a memory in detail we can attach a new anchor - or even a series of them - to it, a new trigger that we can use to release the emotion when and where we want to.

As with most methods in this book, try to gain a good understanding of all the processes behind anchors before you start trying to use them. Note that, on the whole, anchors will only give good results if you've established good rapport. This isn't to say that you can't 'place' anchors without rapport, you can, they just don't work as well.

But please, use these techniques with respect for your subjects. It's just as easy to create a harmful or destructive anchor as it is to create a constructive and positive one. You should always stay well clear of implementing potentially negative anchors and never venture beyond what you feel your abilities can handle, as you are in *a very real sense*, rewiring neurological channels within the brain.

Let's drop anchor...

...And start off nice and slowly by creating an emotional anchor in yourself so that you can get first hand experience of what the fuss is all about. Once established, this anchor will trigger a strong positive, confident emotional state within you that you'll be able to release whenever you feel the need to use it, such as before a performance. Obviously, you can use the following method to elicit an emotional response in others too.

Follow each step below slowly, don't be tempted to just give it a half-hearted try. If you can't give it your best shot right now then don't do it at all, that way you're going to get a much better experience when you do have more time to experiment.

- Think back to a situation when you were full of confidence and self-belief. This could be a point on stage where things were going really well, or an occasion where you won a prize or completed a task - anything, as long as it's a situation where you felt yourself bursting with as much confidence, self-belief and success as possible.

If you don't have a memory like that then the solution is simply to...make one up! Pick a situation you can really relate to, anything that has meaning to you. If you're into football, think what it must be like to be the captain of the team winning the World Cup for example. Think about how you would really feel, what you would look like if you were there, radiating confidence and self-belief as you hold the 'Cup aloft. See the crowd in your mind, hear them roar as you stand at the centre of the field. Feel the shirt you wear, wet with sweat, see the blue sky above you. Feel your power and pride swell. The more completely you can create this scene in your head the more powerful the feelings we'll be able to use in the next stage.

Got a pleasant remembered or imagined memory we can work with now? Good - let's continue.

- Imagine yourself in your chosen scenario and experience it through your own eyes. Relive it. Don't experience it by seeing yourself from the outside. Experience the memory by being inside yourself, looking out through your own eyes. If you find you're having trouble with broadening your memory of the event, start with whatever small details you can remember first. Simple things like what you might have been wearing. Was it day or night? Who else was there? Vivid memories are those where you can recall a lot of lesser details that will in turn trigger more anchors and a deeper recollection of the overall event.

Note that memories of some feelings of confidence can be very short if they're of the 'holding the World Cup aloft' variety. You get a general pleasure from the overall memory, but the strong buzz that you get as you actually remember raising the Cup is only a short burst. If you 'over-remember' this central part of the event you can reduce its strength, you just wont get the same kind of 'hit' out of it if you keep on playing with it. With that in mind, it will help if you can first try to clearly envisage the events *leading up to* the core event. When these memories are clear, then continue on to the culmination of the situation. This way you can ensure the biggest emotional hit from the core memory and therefore the biggest response from this anchor when it's used later on.

- Make a real effort to see, hear, feel and even smell what you experienced that day. Maybe the sight of happy people, the sound of laughter and that happy, intoxicating, tingling sensation of success running down your spine. What do you see? What can you hear? How does your body feel? Close your eyes if you feel that helps you. You can even try to put yourself in the same body position you used that day, or simply adopt the body language you feel would emphasise the confidence and success you felt at that moment (for more on building confidence see the chapter, 'In Daily Life). Take your time. Relive the memory step by step. Take in all the things you remember from that day and let them grow into a kind of daydream state where you feel you could almost be there.

- Whether the positive emotions that you now remember/create most strongly come as a short-lived burst or a longer sense of accomplishment, when they peak close your right hand into a fist and squeeze as hard as you can. Not before they peak, not after - exactly AS they peak. Make a fist and squeeze as you feel this emotion and direct it, focussing on the idea that you're bursting with confidence and success. SQUEEZE!!!!

- Okay, stop for a minute and clear your head. Now go back into the memory again and immerse yourself in it completely. Again relive it, but this time imagine that what you feel is ten times stronger than before. Ten times the confidence, ten times the success. Ten times everything. Let the emotion grow...and grow...and when you feel it's peaking close your right hand into a fist and *squeeze*!! Let the emotion explode as you do this. Ten times stronger than before, SQUEEZE!!! as the feeling peaks.

- Stop. Clear your head and rest for a minute or two. It feels kind of good, doesn't it? Okay, now we want you to relive the memory once more, only this time make the feelings you get from it even stronger. This is the biggest, happiest, most positive feeling you have ever had. The bigger you can make this, the better the result will be. Build up to the core experience, get ready for that single moment when your heart soars and your body feels electric - and when it peaks, *squeeze*!!!! While you do this don't just mentally *say* the word 'squeeze', but scream it out in your head.

- Stop. Completely relax your mind and body. Congratulations, you have just established a very useful anchor within yourself.

Now try the following:

- Wait a short time before trying this out, think about other things for a little while, letting your mind and body relax and settle for a few minutes. When you feel 'neutral' again get ready to trigger the anchor. If you think it'll help to close your eyes as you do this then feel free to do so.

- When you're ready, close your right fist and squeeze, screaming out the word 'SQUEEZE!!!!!!' inside your mind. Keep your hand tightly closed and the word (and nothing but the word!) ringing deafeningly inside your head for at least couple of seconds.

Whoa...! What was that?!? The sudden emotion you just felt was produced by a trick of human neurology that allows you to connect an emotion to a memory, quickly and easily. Cool isn't it? You're actually capable of programming your mind to set off any emotions you want at your command! Just think about the potential of that for a little while...

If you took the easy route and just read the above exercise instead of actually doing it, I suggest you go back and really give it a go. What's to come will be much easier to understand that way.

If your anchor wasn't as powerful as you had expected, take another look at how vivid the images you based the anchor on were. Were you really feeling the entire event as though you were there - or at least strongly enough to give you strong emotions from the memory of it? It's important to be fully immersed in the memory, to live it. If you experience it from the outside, half-remembering it as short snatches of key events it will not work. This is an important lesson to bear in mind when you start trying to establish anchors in other people. They must be fully immersed in what they're feeling.

Did you also really set the anchor when the feeling peaked? Not when it was about to peak or just after, but *when it peaked*?!!?

In the example above we actually created two anchors: a tactile one (the squeezing of the hand) and a vocal one (the word 'squeeze'). Not so strangely, you'll get the deepest feelings from this exercise when you trigger the anchors in the same order you created them in. In the example above the tactile anchor is triggered first and then the vocal one. The order you first create, then trigger the anchors in is integral to the whole structure of the anchor system, so take care to release them in the correct way.

In application on other people, you shouldn't be as obvious as we were in the exercise above and the anchor or anchors you place should be so subtle that your participant will never consciously know what you're doing. Subconsciously though, they'll register it all completely! It's been proven that subtle subconscious anchors work far better than obvious ones, so don't think that you have to go overboard creating big demonstrative release signals every time.

Preferred Anchors

In the same way that we all have our preferred way of receiving information (tactile, vocal, etc) we have preferred anchors too.

When you use anchors on volunteers, for maximum effect the 'releaser' (first anchor) you create should match their favoured primary system. If for example you've found that your subject is very visual then you can use a drawn symbol as a trigger, if they're more affected by aural stimuli then use a word or sound.

As we don't know which system you yourself respond most quickly to, we chose to use here the one that most people react well to, namely the tactile system. If you're still not up to speed about recognising your subject's favoured primary system and still want to try this out, we'd advise you to also go for the tactile system - we all use it to some extent and almost everyone will respond well to tactile anchors. For added effect we've also introduced a vocal anchor into the example and, with these two in play together, most of you will easily be able to feel a strong, positive shift in your emotions from this exercise.

If you know your own primary system then change the exercise to suit it and you'll see what a real difference it makes.

Strengthening the Imagery

The power of anchors lies in the fact that we don't have to seek out the subject's memories to make use of their emotional content, we can just as easily create an imaginary setting, complete with emotional impact, and make use of that instead. It's far easier than you might think to talk people into creating a vivid imaginary setting for themselves. They'll be able to do a good job of imagining most scenarios, but if you're clever you can help them add in other details they might not have considered to make their images even stronger. Analyse the setting you want them to imagine beforehand and make certain you know as much as you can about what it would be like in real life. Be your subject's imagination, take the stress off him and talk about what he might smell, how his feet feel in his shoes, the clothes he's wearing, the weather. All the things he might not have considered for himself. Asking abstract things about how his feet feel or whether or not his hands are sweating are not just there to add fine detail, but help to give unique depth to the created scene.

And why stop with just creating 'confidence' anchors? Mix the use of suggestion with anchors and you can take this anywhere. For example, all modern research shows that being successful as a sportswoman/man is closely linked to self-image and positivity. Athletes could easily create mental images of being stronger, faster and with more endurance, anchoring these feelings to a snap of their fingers. Who wouldn't benefit from the sudden surge of confidence this would give?

Anchors - a programmable, instantly accessible source of confidence, available to anyone.

Developing Anchors

You can easily build upon an existing anchor to make it even stronger. If you take the anchor we've just created as an example, you could amplify its effects by simply anchoring it to a second memory where the subject has again experienced extreme confidence. There is no limit to the amount of positive events you can link a single 'confidence response' to.

Martin: "To give you an example of using anchors outside the boundaries of mentalism, I'm a certified Dive Master, regularly working with instructors and newly qualified students. If there's a diver who seems nervous about their first dive I usually set them a 'confidence anchor' before going into the water. Just before they make the dive I trigger the anchor, making the person relax and generally have a much more enjoyable and less stressful time.

"When we get out of the water I like to re-anchor to the 'high' the diver is feeling; a good first dive is a very powerful mix of adrenaline, success, happiness and general well-being that I can link to the already existing anchor. So in a way you can go from a functional self-created anchor to a "super" anchor with this technique. There is no limit to how strong you can make an anchor by layering new positive experiences on top of it to re-anchor to."

The same rules apply to your own 'confidence anchor', so remember to re-anchor it to even more positive emotions when the opportunities arise.

The Structure of an Anchor

Let's now look at what triggers you might use in your performance to create an anchor.

Visual anchors:

Visual anchors are easy to put in place in a stage setting, using hand and/or head movements or big, simple images on flash cards. Anchors work best if the trigger for them is instantly memorable. If you do use flash cards, try to make the symbols or images upon them striking and unusual for greater impact.

- A wave of your hand in front of your participants eyes.

- Place your participant with eyes closed in front of any image or symbol you want to use as the trigger and have them open their eyes at the moment the emotion peaks.

Tactile anchors:

Tactile anchors are great. They usually work really well and are easy to implement, so if you're a mentalist we'd suggest that they're what you'll be making most use of. Examples of tactile anchors could be (again placed at the moment the emotion peaks):

- A light squeeze on your participants shoulders.
- A tap on the participant's knee.
- Brushing your hand gently across their hand/s.
- As in the earlier exercise, getting the subject to squeeze their hand.

Of course you can also use smells and tastes as anchors too. As we said earlier, smells in particular are incredibly evocative for most people, so if you can introduce an anchor linked to an odour it will tend to work very well. The reason for this is that a lot of our primal instincts are still linked closely to our olfactory sense. The area in our brain which we use to recognise odours is really ridiculously large when you consider that our actual ability to smell (compared to most other members of the animal kingdom) is very limited. Small as our range is, what we *can* smell creates rapid subconscious effects in every one of us, changing our emotions long before our conscious minds noticed any odour was present.

Aural/Vocal anchors:

Vocal anchors are powerful too. They're easy to create and great to use both on their own or combined with other systems (more about that in a second). Examples of vocal anchors might be:
- a word
- a sentence
- a sound
- a melody

Combining anchors

An example of combining anchors would be where you have your hand on a participant's shoulder and, as you establish the anchor peak, you gently press the shoulder and turn your head at the same time, establishing both a tactile and a visual anchor. Of course, anchors that have multiple triggers are much deeper and provoke speedier reactions than those using one.

An example of a three-sense anchor might be to again gently squeeze the subject's shoulder while you bring your other hand up to your mouth and cough. This will of course create a tactile anchor (squeeze of the shoulder), a visual anchor (bringing your hand to your mouth) and a vocal anchor (the coughing). If you hit three systems at once - and if the fundamentals are in place - you'll have instigated a very powerful anchor.

One anchor - multiple systems:

It's also possible to use one single anchor that can be recognised and therefore triggered through two or more senses at once. An example could be to use the drumming of your fingers as an anchor. It's both very visual and aural (the rhythmic sound of your fingertips hitting the table) and can therefore be triggered by just seeing or hearing you do it again. Multiple anchors like these will normally work even better than anchors that are triggered through just one system.

The Anchored Card Projection

Martin: "Here's an easy routine I've used on numerous occasions with great success using just an olfactory anchor. Although I explain this as a 'psychic' effect here, you can of course use whatever scripting suits your own style."

Set up

Take five playing cards and place a LIGHT dab of after-shave or perfume on one of them. we really do mean a light dab here, leaving a subtle aroma so light that you have to smell the card closely to notice it.

Tell the audience that it's long been known that psychic ability increases exponentially as the other senses have been disabled. You would now like to demonstrate this...!

Place the five cards face down on a table, noting what position the 'olfactory' card is in.

It's an idea to use Zenner cards (a five symbol deck that's normally used for testing ESP) for this, justifying why there are only five cards to choose from. If you were to use normal playing cards the audience will begin to wonder (unless you've shown that you've taken them at random from a deck) exactly why you've chosen these particular cards and not other values.

Call up two participants and blindfold one, ensuring that he or she can't see anything and making sure that the audience is convinced that this is so.

With their sense of sight now disabled, your subject's other senses now really will be much more acute than they were; primarily though they'll become much more reliant on their sense of hearing. You therefore need to direct them away from hearing into exploring all of their other senses, in particular their sense of smell, without actually saying that this is what you want them to do. The easiest way to do this is to take the subject through a very quick relaxation process (see the later chapter, 'Relaxation') that culminates with the subject's attention being focussed mainly on their breathing. Ideally you want their breathing to be slow and low in their abdomen rather than in their upper chest as most people do.

Explain to the subject and the audience that you will now pick up one of the five cards at random - but of course you will choose the olfactory card. Put this card in the participant's hand and ask them to hold it in front of their forehead, making sure that they hold it with the face side outwards towards the audience so that they can see it clearly.

Now tell the volunteer to that you're going to try to project the image of the card to him or her and that it's important that they keep it close to their forehead (even at their 'third eye' if that fits in with your style) to get a strong psychic impression of it.

"Stay relaxed, let images and impressions flood in from all your other senses. Explore everything you feel, still breathing slowly and gently...let this card grow in your mind above all others. You don't have to visually see it's value in your mind's eye, just try to get an overall sense of the presence that this particular card has...don't worry about the number. Just be open to how the card feels to you in every way."

Allow them to do this. Now take the card from them and (with the subject still blindfolded) put it face down on the table with the other four cards. Now ask the other volunteer to mix up the five cards and turn them all face up.

When this is done take the blindfold off participant 'A' and tell them to take up one card at a time, holding it in front of his or her forehead just as before to see if they can sense which card they had held previously; they can close their eyes if they feel this will help. Tell the subject not to say anything or make any decisions about which card is which until they've gone through all of them.

When the subject has done that, tell them to look at the cards and use their intuition to decide which card you tried to project to them. Tell him/her that if they think rationally about it they - and you - will fail. They must only use their intuition.

"Look at the cards. Which card feels right? Pick it up NOW!"

You'll be surprised (or by now, probably not) when the subject chooses the correct card. Because of the anchor, they subconsciously recognise the subtle smell on the card and, if they really let their intuition decide instead of using conscious reasoning, they will pick up the right card on most occasions.

Because it *is* such a subtle smell and therefore easy to miss, this routine is by no means 100% (though very close). But then again what is? It makes for a daring, perplexing effect that's a lot of fun to do. From the audience's point of view everything will seem perfectly fair and your volunteer will not consciously notice or comment on any smell (if you haven't gone overboard with the after-shave that is).

You can easily change this effect to make it suit your style as it works as a powerful one on one mental routine too. You could let the subject find the card when it's face down for example; you'll get a nice 'wow' effect out of your audience when the correct card is chosen without even knowing what its value is!

You could also do it with more than one spectator, making an extremely powerful moment when you reveal that three subjects have chosen the same 'mentally projected' card without knowing or seeing what the others have taken. Just remove their blindfolds one at a time and go through the routine one by one on each of them. You could even use something other than cards, such as a range of small objects. This really has endless possibilities. Be creative - what's the worst thing that can happen?

If you want to up the odds and make this effect as close to infallible as it can be, again have a look in Banacheck´s, 'Psychological Subtleties' and implement his thoughts from the 'subtle cards' section. Do this and you really are as close to perfect as anyone needs to be."

The Fundamentals of Successful Anchoring

Just to re-cap, the fundamentals for successful anchoring are listed here. If you take these few 'musts' to heart and practise what you've read so far you'll soon be wondering how you've been able to live without this skill.

Rapport.

Remember that you must have established good rapport before attempting to establish an anchor. You could argue that you can place an anchor despite not having good rapport and, as we said earlier, we're sure you can; but it will work miserably.

Which system?
As you begin to create rapport with the participant it should be fairly easy to recognise which systems they respond best to. Establish which primary system your subject prefers and USE IT!! This will give a faster, deeper and more easily implemented anchor. Use anchors from across the range of *all* preferred systems and also use multiple anchors where possible.

Make your anchor unique and striking.
Making your anchor unique allows your subjects to recognise it more quickly and with less chance of confusion. If you use a general or vague and unremarkable anchor that might occur at any point in any average conversation it may not be noticed.

Fully associate with the emotion.
By this we mean that the person should be coaxed into actually trying to be one with the scenario they're using to create the desired emotion. You're not asking them just to remember something, but to actually relive it. For an anchor to work, the subject(s) have to be as involved as possible with the emotion they're experiencing. This really is a must if you want to create a successful anchor.

The reason for this is of course because it makes what the person is experiencing a whole lot more intense. If the subject just watches themselves in the memory 'from the outside' rather than reliving it, they have no emotional investment in this remembered reality and there'll be no anchor to create, hold or eventually release.

A successful anchor is created
when the subject's emotions peak.
That more or less says it all. You must create your anchor when the emotion peaks. Not when it is about to peak or when it has just peaked, but AS it peaks. Obviously, you'll not be capturing

the full emotional potential to base your anchor on if it's at any other time.

How to decide when an emotion is peaking? Easy - you evaluate the person in front of you with the tools you've already learned in the first couple of chapters. Check breathing, eye movements, size of pupil, facial expression, skin tone, voice, etc. You can also, in the right circumstances, get away with just asking the subject outright when they're feeling the emotion most strongly. Get them to shout a loud 'Now!', or as before, 'Squeeze!', it'll add another vocal and tactile anchor to the ones you're already building, making it much stronger.

Release structure of anchors.

When using more than one anchor, remember to release them in the order they were placed in. For instance if you've implemented a vocal anchor followed by a visual anchor you must release them in that order. The sequence they're created in is an integral part of their whole makeup. To release them in any other way disrupts the structure of the anchor and renders it useless.

Primary anchor first

Always release the primary anchor first. You'll get far better results that way.

Repetition matters.

To build a deep and effective anchor you need to repeat the creation stage - and repeat it correctly on each occasion - as many times as you can. Three or four is usually the maximum anyone can do before they run out of energy and can't go another step higher; but if you can get away with more repetitions, do them.

Obviously an anchor created and left *without* repetition, but created in accordance with the above rules, will work fine; BUT it will not be as deep or last as long as an anchor which has successfully been planted a number of times.

6

Relaxation

Are you relaxed? Can you understand how to relax others if you aren't? Although this might be seen as a big departure from mentalism, there are a lot of reasons to learn how to relax yourself and others quickly. For example, getting some subjects to relax (and therefore do as you say competently) at all is nigh on impossible in some cases. Although their presence as your volunteer does indicate that they're more outgoing and less nervy than most, once actually in the glare of the metaphorical spotlight even the best subjects can seize up. If they aren't relaxed they'll have little focus, so no attention to what you're telling them to do.

For most of us, relaxing properly is a lot harder than it sounds. Even when we're sure that we're physically quite relaxed we're still full of subtle tensions that prevent us from being *completely* relaxed. Although you might not be able to feel it right now, every thought you have creates a minute (and sometimes not so minute!) physical stress somewhere in your body. You might suppose that it's fairly innocuous to think of the past or future - but, just as you sub-vocalise when you read, when you remember past events or anticipate future ones, your body and mind react in the same way as they would during the real situation. If for example you were vividly imagining talking through a speech you were about to give, to some extent that would create the same movements of your diaphragm and Adam's Apple, even the same emotions and physical tensions as giving the real speech would. You can never 'just' think. When you think you 'do' too.

Your intensity of thought directly affects your attainable level of relaxation. This plays a major role in creating your mood at every point in the day with, as you might assume, remembering negative events creating the strongest physical and mental tensions in you. Luckily, learning to relax lessens the power of negative emotions by 'smoothing out' the physical effects they create. Once these are gone the negative emotion has nothing sustaining it in a physical sense, so is much shorter lived.

Points & Chakras

Relaxing is as much about learning *where* to relax as how to, and it will obviously help if you can learn to identify the main places on your body that tense up when you do think. Many people can go through their entire lives with one or more or of these places 'locked up' with a permanent subtle tension. The most common point to restrict in this way is the one at your solar plexus, which can just as easily be made tense by things like sitting in a bad posture as by remembering something unpleasant. If you work in an office where you sit most of the time, or you drive for a living, there's a strong possibility that you're restricting this point every day and affecting how you feel. People who are restricted at the solar plexus tend to have periods of anxiety without any apparent cause, feel vulnerable, find it hard to enjoy things and generally can't relax fully.

Other people might be tense at the throat or abdomen, sometimes because of anger or insecurity. And the problem is that the longer you feel tense at these points the longer you *will* feel angry or insecure. Physical tensions created by negative emotions create and perpetuate those very same emotions. If you can learn to turn off the tensions then you're going a long way towards removing the emotions too.

Some of the primary points of tension below correspond to what are called 'Chakras' in Hindu and Buddhist meditation, but we wont explore Chakras in any great detail in this book and they wont require your belief in them in their full esoteric sense to appreciate their action. Don't try to imagine them as being anything in particular for now, just learn to be able to locate and relax them.

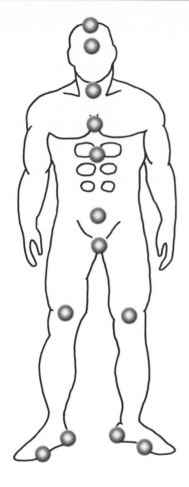

Figure 2 - Points & Chakras

Starting from the ground upwards, you can find primary relaxation points and Chakras (where stated) - at:

- The centre of the sole of each foot at the same horizontal level as the peak of the arch of your foot.
- The centre of each heel (relax the ankles to help find this one)
- Behind the knees.
- **Mooldhara or Root Chakra**, at the perineum.
- **Swadistana or Sacrum Chakra**, on the abdomen, three finger widths below the navel.

- **Manipura or Solar Plexus Chakra**, at the solar plexus under the upturned 'V' of the ribs.
- **Anahata or Heart Chakra**. Place your hand flat and horizontally on your chest with the tip of your little finger on your Solar Plexus point. Your first finger should now be lying horizontally over your Heart Chakra. When working with this Chakra, make certain that you aren't accidentally concentrating on a secondary point between it and your solar plexus. Doing so will create tension and sometimes feelings of anxiety too.
- **Visuddhi or Throat Chakra**, at the centre of the throat.
- **Ajna or Inner Eye Chakra**, between the eyebrows.
- **Sahashara or Crown Chakra**, four finger widths forward of the crown of your head

Figure 3 - A Standard Chakra Chart

Relaxing Points & Chakras

It's doubtful that anyone would ever have enough time in a performance to go through all of the above, but if you can pay at least some attention to the subject's solar plexus, upper chest points and shoulders it should take the edge of any anxiety or tension they may be feeling.

If you find that you do need to relax subjects deeply for a hypnotic-style routine - and put them at their ease by giving them something they can focus on - try the following routine. You can also use this as a quick way of weeding out those people who aren't going to be able to concentrate well enough to work with.

Ask your subject to hold his/her arm out to the side at shoulder height. Bring your hands up to support it at the wrist and mid-bicep. Ask the volunteer to relax as deeply as possible. When they appear to have done so, whip your supporting arm away from theirs and see what happens. If the arm falls quickly to their side they're relaxed and very likely a good subject too. If you are lucky enough to have at least one subject whose arm does fall quickly, it's a valuable illustration for your other subjects of what deep relaxation really is. As we're all quite empathic, seeing someone else relax is a good role model for us, a visual demonstration of the depth of relaxation we're aiming for. We put ourselves in the place of the person flopping their arm down and suddenly it's apparent how *we* need to do it.

But if you don't have a subject who responds like this as an example and you have to relax your current subject as quickly as you can, work on the higher points as much as time will allow; anything is better than nothing. When speed's of the essence it also helps if you place your hand(s) over or upon the area you want the subject to relax. Also, it will help to fix their eyes with a gaze - steady eyes create a steady mind. Put both hands on/over the subject's shoulders. Let your hands hang a little heavily if you do decide to actually touch the subject, this forces them into reacting quickly (as you would be able to feel it if they were slow in complying) and also makes sure that *both* shoulders relax. "Let your shoulders fall, down, relaxed, your elbows heavy."

Your hand now goes to the back of their neck as you say, "Relax your neck, let your head relax back a little." As you say this you use some forward pressure to allow the subject to rest back in your hand, briefly taking some of the stress off their neck and helping them to let go of tensions there. "Relaxed, let it all go, your neck is soft, relaxed, free."

As it's very common for subjects to relax at the point you're working on but then tense up again the second you move onto somewhere new, move back to the shoulders for a few seconds, reinforcing what you said earlier, "Down, relaxed, falling down. Heavy and relaxed."

For the upper chest and solar plexus it obviously isn't a good idea to actually touch your female subjects. Instead, hold your palm near and facing their throat and slowly lower it a few inches as you say, "Falling, relaxing, slowly opening out like a flower. Relaxing, opening." Though it might sound like just a bit of twee scripting, talking about things 'opening out' is important. Real relaxation at these points, when it's done correctly, gives feelings of opening up, like an eye or mouth, so saying things like this give a sense of what you're trying to convey.

You might go through these same points (neck, shoulders, chest/solar plexus) a couple of times, reinforcing the relaxation commands until you feel confident that the subject has relaxed. At this point you might even want to anchor the experience of complete relaxation so that you can trigger it again later should you need to.

7

Suggestion

Suggestions - *verbal or non-verbal inducements to act or think in ways the hypnotist indicates in an effortless or non-voluntary manner, without criticality.*

Suggestions change how your subject perceives the world and, more importantly, allows you to create the world that you want them to see. Limbs move of their own accord, things twist and writhe in the hand, grow hot, cold or numb - almost any sensation or illusion can be created in the participant's mind. And this can all be done far more easily than you might think. Under the right circumstances if we simply suggest to our subjects that something may happen then, and with very little proof, they will accept that it will really take place. This doesn't make them stupid or gullible, it just shows that belief is based almost entirely on assumption and memory rather than direct experience. It's our nature, our need to survive, that requires us to *have* to believe what our senses tell us. As we have no opportunity to test each perception as it comes into our minds we generally accept what our senses report at face value, regardless of whether they're right or wrong. We can of course as Mentalists make great use of this by either, creating false perceptions - or attribute false causes to real perceptions. In so doing we control what the subject sees and believes.

Suggestions can be given to your subjects in a variety of ways that are usually defined within the following categories:

- **Verbal** - Transmitted by words, for example, via 'hypnotic' suggestion, which we cover in the following chapter.
- **Extra-verbal** - Transmitted indirectly by the *implication* of words, such as through normalisations, omissions and generalisations as we explain below.

- **Intra-verbal** - Transmitted through the modulation of the voice, usually as anchors. See also the later section on 'Echoes'.
- **Non-verbal** - Transmitted by gestures and movements, again via the use of anchors and Echoes.

Let's now take a closer look at the use of words as a means of giving indirect suggestions extra-verbally.

Sleight of mouth - Extra-Verbal Suggestion

'If thoughts can corrupt language, language can also corrupt thoughts.'

- George Orwell

Words. Nothing like them. We can use them to create miracles, to sway, to deceive, to conquer.

Although we'll talk about some aspects of NLP here, we're going to avoid detailing the entire 'sleight of mouth' system as used by NLP practitioners. Instead we'll concentrate solely on those parts of it that we feel will help you learn how to fool as much with the words you use as you do with your tricks themselves. What's here is common sense use of language, just simple good 'handling' that reflects magic performance principles that have been around for years. We fool each other every day with words like this and you probably even consciously use some of these structures yourself already. The point here isn't to sell you any one particular system (such as NLP) and say that it originated this kind of use of words, but simply to highlight the power of language and to make sure you understand its full potential.

The model for 'sleight of mouth' consists of verbal patterns that can be grouped into the following three categories: omissions, generalisations and distortions, which you'll note we use in effects and verbal techniques throughout this book. We'll describe each here briefly and give a general indication of their usage, but will continue to exploit and broaden each element as we go along.

Omissions - Letting the subject decide what's taking place.

Often two people talk about the same subject but are communicating from their respective knowledge of it without ensuring that the other person understands what's being said. We all have a tendency to unconsciously assume that whoever we're speaking to fully understands what we're talking about. For instance we might say, "This is a much better pie!" But better than which pie and why?

We as mentalists can (and do) use omissions in a variety of circumstances. In a sentence like, "You can feel it happening inside your hand!", what can they feel happening? Without telling the subject what 'it' is they're left to define the expected sensations themselves. With these words you plant notions of (non-existent) feelings occurring in the hand of a participant simply by using an 'incomplete' sentence and letting their mind do the rest.

The more accurately you describe what the outcome of any routine will be, the more you're bound to having make sure that it will take place. But broad statements like, "you'll get a strange feeling when I do 'X'" allows masses of leeway for other things to occur and to be assumed to be the desired outcome of the trick.

If you were to say, "Many people experience the same weird feelings that you are experiencing," what is the weird feeling? Who says the participant is experiencing anything at all? And, as we'll see later, would they really contradict this statement if they weren't?

Generalisations - people *always* use them...

Words such as: all, always, never, everything, nobody, etc., are what we call 'Universal Generalisations'. In the phrase, "Many people experience the same weird feelings that you are experiencing," the, 'Many people' part is a generalisation that would make a subject believe that you'd not only done this trick a number of times, but that it's also been *successful* many times.

Another universal generalisation would be, "It's well known that *all* mentalists posses a certain degree of psychic powers". All? How ridiculous is that? But, coming from a mentalist this universal generalisation may be taken at face value and will help emphasise that what you do is based on paranormal skills (if that's what you're trying to promote yourself as having).

Generalisations are used creatively by everybody from politicians down (if there IS a 'down' from being a politician☺) to give weight to what they're saying and give the impression that whatever facts they're trying to promote are commonly accepted (or not) by most of the rest of the World. "Everybody knows that." Or, "You *always* want this..." Everybody? Always? And the thing is that these words get overlooked in daily conversations and are 'hardly ever' contradicted.

If you say, "There are many people who think that the following routine I am about to attempt is far too dangerous to do in public, but...," you've created the illusion that what you're about to do isn't approved of by someone, somewhere who's supposed opinion on the trick actually matters; thus creating anticipation and an edgy tension without having even begun to do anything by way of an effect.

Martin: "Countering a negative statement, such as a generalisation made by a member of the onlookers about themselves, can be a real opportunity to get the subject and the rest of the spectators on your side. If an audience member said to me, "I'm *never* used as a participant !", this is a perfect statement to do something with; not least of all because this statement infers that the participant has always hoped to be used in this way and therefore will make a willing subject. I'd direct my attention towards this person and say something along the lines of, "Yes - I know! I feel it's because you seem very confident and at peace with yourself - much more so than others I meet. I think many people pick up on this subconsciously and leave you be because of it." Obviously this is complete nonsense, but the participant will tend to agree and eat this flattery up. I, the 'great mind reader', have in my infinite wisdom actually seen this person for who he/she really is.

Continue along the lines of, "I'd like to try an experiment with you if you wouldn't mind? I think it could prove very interesting with a person with your qualities"; and you've just created a very happy and compliant subject who feels valued by you. An added bonus is that the people watching have also just seen you assess an unknown participant's character absolutely perfectly - because didn't he or she just say that you were right in what you said about them?"

Of course, as a tool for cold reading, there's nothing like a few generalisations and a little flattery slipped into your script to give the impression that you know far more about someone than you really do. It also helps to make a statement and give its antithesis at the same time, so you can't help but be right. You might say, "Because of your past, you can sometimes be very guarded about your feelings, but in the right situation you blossom and can be far too open and sincere, allowing people to take advantage of you." Doesn't that cover just about everyone you've ever met? And saying, 'Because of your past...', will create the assumption that you know what the subject's past is.

In a series of experiments carried out by psychologist B.R. Forer in the '40's, Forer found that people will usually accept generalisations about their personalities without ever considering that the same description could be given of almost anybody. He devised this classic 'cold-reading' script (that's based almost entirely of Generalisations and Omissions) and asked volunteers to rate its accuracy as an assessment of their character:-

'You have a need for other people to like and admire you, and yet you tend to be critical of yourself. While you have some personality weaknesses you are generally able to compensate for them. You have considerable unused capacity that you have not turned to your advantage. Disciplined and self-controlled on the outside, you tend to be worrisome and insecure on the inside. At times you have serious doubts as to whether you have made the right decision or done the right thing. You prefer a certain amount of change and variety and become dissatisfied when hemmed in by restrictions and limitations. You also pride yourself as an independent thinker; and do not accept others' statements without satisfactory proof. But you have found it unwise to be too frank in revealing yourself to others. At times you are extroverted, affable, and sociable, while at other times you are introverted, wary, and reserved. Some of your aspirations tend to be rather unrealistic.'

Forer's subjects then scored this evaluation from 0 to 5, with a score of '5' indicating that the recipient felt it was 'excellent' assessment and '4' meaning the assessment was 'good', and so on down to 0. The average evaluation score given by the volunteers was 4.26 and, despite being repeated hundreds of times in research centres around the globe since it's inception in 1948, the average score given for the text as an accurate reflection of *anyone's* character still remains at about 4.2.

We can't help but believe things that are said about us that portray us as we would like to be seen. We'll accept doubtful and even overtly and obviously untrue statements if they're flattering enough or fit in with our own self-image, be that positive or negative.

Normalisations:
Saying nothing whilst appearing to say something.

Normalisations leave out so much information from a sentence that there's almost nothing of substance left. For example, in the sentence, "We need to discuss the difficult situation concerning essential components within the mentalist process". If you don't take too much notice on your first reading this could come across as a fair statement. But if you think about it for any length of time you'll realise that it says almost nothing at all. 'Difficult situation.' What situation? Why is it difficult? 'Essential components'. What components? Why are they essential? Etc, etc.

Normalisations help you avoid describing routines before or as you do them and are an excellent form of misdirection. Without a definition of what any particular routine entails, subjects and spectators become confused as they try to grasp what has been said, which puts them off-kilter enough to guide them away from what the performer might be doing elsewhere. Also, if - through use of normalisations - the audience has no idea what the outcome of a trick is meant to be, if it goes wrong the performer has the opportunity of disguising this by moving into another routine instead.

Anchors, Intra-Verbal & Non-Verbal Suggestion.

Although suggestions can be anchored to simple word stresses (and of course gestures, etc.) very effectively, there is of course a limit to the extent of 'commands' you can deliver by this method. Some people would have you believe that stressing words and phrases within nonsensical sentences like the following is usable subliminal/hypnotic suggestion that will elicit all kinds of wonderful effects:

"...And, if **YOU** were to turn to the end of the other side of the stage, you know that people can **FEEL** in ways that are **VERY** prone to moving them into the end of a **SLEEPY** day."

But if you want to have your subject respond to your suggestions they either have to be very be clear and concise, or repeated and reinforced regularly - or both. With sentences like the above, who's to say that the subject has even noticed these suggestions? And what reason have you given him or her to comply with them?

Have a conversation with someone and you'll notice very quickly that whilst the other person's speaking you're thinking about what *you* want to say and all manner of other things; with only a small part of your awareness concerned with what the person is saying . Because of that, unless you've made certain that you have your subject's full attention, he or she is liable to miss all of your subtle suggestions.

Unless the human consciousness is primed to look for and respond to particular ideas, just saying selected sequences of words can't work as 'suggestion' in the usual sense, because the mind is just too busy to take them on board. Conversely, if they *are* paying a lot of attention and you continually use sentences like the above, pretty soon your subjects become very consciously aware of what you're trying to do. The nonsense is seen to be nonsense and the 'subliminal' commands become obvious and ineffective. But we *can* use this type of effect to some degree, albeit in a lesser form, to help force a subject, say, towards choosing a particular object. Why this works in the way it does is pretty straightforward in that our minds tend to repeat or 'echo' any stimuli that they've been made aware of. The greater the stimuli and the more emotion you associate with it, the stronger the echo. Loud and frequent at first, echoes slowly die away as new information comes into the brain and supersedes them.

A perfect example of mental 'echoes' are when you can't get a particular tune out of your head. On your first hearing of the song, by repetition it's chorus becomes embedded in your subconscious. You hum it as snatches of it come back to you over the next hours, allowing it to become more and more deeply embedded in your memory. With further exposure to the song you can end up with a continual echo, a stream of thought filling the edges of your subconscious that's almost constantly humming the tune for days at a time. You might occassionally escape and think about other things for a while, but the more often you've heard the song the more likely it is to echo - and you end up humming it all over again.

We can have 'echos' of anything: a sound, an image, a sensation, any stimuli that leaves a strong impression on our senses. See striking clothes you like/dislike in a shop window as you go by in a car and you'll have recurring flashes of the clothes for a few seconds after you've passed by. Echos are more or less neutral if they're caused by say, the the sight of a flower; but the more emotional content that's associated with them the stronger they are and the longer they will last. If you associate a song with sad event for example - and hear it often enough - the song can trigger sadness, or sadness will trigger a memory of the song.

Helped along by natural processes such as echoes, linguistic suggestion requires no 'trance' or special state to have an effect, just clever delivery and good scripting. Many popular mentalists make a good living from using it well, so consider; is what you say in any routine as clear as it could be? Is it conversely as *ambiguous and deceitful* as it could be? Could you maximise the effect of your routines by employing a more creative use of language?

8

Hypnosis & Suggestion

Hypnosis typically involves an introduction to the procedure during which the subject is told that suggestions for imaginative experiences will be presented. The hypnotic induction is an extended initial suggestion for using one's imagination, and may contain further elaborations of the introduction. A hypnotic procedure is used to encourage and evaluate responses to suggestions. When using hypnosis, one person (the subject) is guided by another (the hypnotist) to respond to suggestions for changes in subjective experience, alterations in perception, sensation, emotion, thought or behavior. Persons can also learn self-hypnosis, which is the act of administering hypnotic procedures on one's own. If the subject responds to hypnotic suggestions, it is generally inferred that hypnosis has been induced. Many believe that hypnotic responses and experiences are characteristic of a hypnotic state. While some think that it is not necessary to use the word "hypnosis" as part of the hypnotic induction, others view it as essential.

Details of hypnotic procedures and suggestions will differ depending on the goals of the practitioner and the purposes of the clinical or research endeavor. Procedures traditionally involve suggestions to relax, though relaxation is not necessary for hypnosis and a wide variety of suggestions can be used including those to become more alert.

- This definition and description of hypnosis was prepared by the **Executive Committee of the American Psychological Association, Division of Psychological Hypnosis.**

Hypnosis as a whole is both less *and* more powerful than most people understand it to be. It isn't an infallible method of retrieving lost memories, recalling past lives, or curing all illnesses - but it *is* a tool that allows you to access the power of the mind to *help* heal both physically and mentally. Here however, as deceitful as it may be, we're simply going to use it to cheat and mislead!

It's a very common belief that hypnosis can help recover and/or enhance memories. Although there've been many occasions where say, police forces have tried to use it to discover new details of a crime someone might have witnessed, this rarely leads to the retrieval of information other than what the subject could already recall whilst awake. Being 'hypnotised' will simply tend to make a subject more creative, causing them to fill in any gaps in what he or she has seen with imagined details. A subject will rarely do this on purpose; the relationship between the hypnotist and subject can be a strange one, where the subject will do everything he can to please the hypnotist and provide him with the information the subject thinks he desires. This is more than enough reason for the British judicial system (and most others around the world) not to accept information gained under hypnosis.

As the psychologist R.W White points out, the goal for the hypnotic subject is to, '...behave like a hypnotised person as this is continuously defined by the operator (the hypnotist) and understood by the subject.' He and many others believe that the subject's motive is, "...submission to the operator's demands. He understands at all times what the operator intends, and his behaviour is a striving to put these intentions into execution."

And as Ormond McGill writes in his book, 'An Encyclopaedia of Stage Hypnotism', "...the subject will also strive to please the audience as much, or more so, than he might the hypnotist."

The very best of all subjects are obviously then those in whom fulfilling the desires of the hypnotist and/or the audience is the strongest. But this subconscious urge to give the hypnotist what he hopes to find has created endless problems for hypnotherapists, most recently in Europe in cases of 'Satanic' or parental abuse in children and in America with the emergence of the idea of 'Alien Abduction'. Look for evidence of aliens, child-abusers or past lives in the right subject and you will co-operatively create that evidence with them. Despite the objections of many hypnotists (particularly those working with 'alien abduction'), people can very easily be 'led' during hypnosis into saying and believing all kinds of things that have never taken place. If you were trying to find out if your subject had been abducted by aliens for example, you might describe the subject lying in bed prior to the 'abduction event'. You eagerly and unwittingly say at one point, "Can you see any strange lights in your room, or anything else unusual?" Nine times out of ten the subject will subconsciously understand that lights are what you're looking for and reply, "yes!" Ask them too if there are any hospital-type tables, equipment or aliens in the room and you'll get all of those things and more. If not the subject will feel that he or she has failed the hypnotist - and in some cases, that they have lost out on an opportunity to get their '15 minutes of fame'.

In 'regressional hypnosis', taking the subject back to another point in his/her life (or into a supposed 'previous life'), the opportunities for the subject and hypnotist to create a mutual delusion are far more extensive. It's very telling, that a high proportion of those regressed to a past life will turn out to have been a priestess, prince or pirate, rather than a lowly worker in a Diner somewhere in this previous existence.

Even the most respected instances of regressional hypnosis discovering a former life, such as the infamous case of Bridey Murphy, eventually fall apart upon examination. When Morey Bernstein, a local businessman and amateur hypnotist, tried to find evidence of a past incarnation in Virginia Tighe of Colorado in 1952, Tighe soon began to recount vivid tales of her former existence as one Bridey Murphy, who had lived in 19th century Ireland. She spoke in an authentic Irish brogue, sang old Irish songs and described events from her former life that nobody believed could be fabricated by anyone without real first-hand knowledge. The stories she told were rich and detailed, driving Bernstein to hypnotise her again and again over many months.

Once news about his discovery got out, Bernstein was encouraged to release recordings of their hypnosis sessions, which were translated into more than a dozen languages and snapped up by a public eager to have proof of the continuance of the soul from one incarnation to the next. With the publication of Bernstein's work, 'The Search for Bridey Murphy' (where Tighe is called 'Ruth Simmons'), the world saw a boom in interest in reincarnation, spawning a series of supposed similar cases and endless books for years thereafter.

However, when newspaper reporters eventually investigated the case they didn't find a Bridey Murphy living in 19th century Ireland, but one in 20th century Wisconsin instead. Just across the street from Tighe's childhood home in Wisconsin had lived one Bridie Murphey Corkell, an old Irish immigrant and friend of the Tighes, who supplied almost every detail of Tighe's 'previous life'. It remains unknown whether Tighe purposely used and added to the stories she had heard and later repeated, but probably not. If a hypnotist asks a good subject to remember a past life then the subject will try to do just that, calling on every memory and experience to create an acceptable reality for the hypnotist. With 'past lives regression' there's an open stage for the subject to become exactly who he wants to be seen as, to create a past for himself that says that once, in some way, he was more than the person he appears to be now. With the hypnotist consciously or subconsciously helping along, why shouldn't they together find what they both hope to discover?

Some hypnotists even try to treat ailments that are supposedly responses to injuries and stresses we received in past lives. For example, a bullet wound gained in one life turns into a cancer in the next. Though a pretty creative idea - and one that there's no direct evidence for - again it's building the possibility of leading into it's own methodology.

There are even those who claim to work on the person you are (or aren't?) *between* lives too, for '...people interested in achieving an experiential understanding of their nature as an eternal spiritual being through the process of Life-Between-Lives Spiritual Regression', no less!

Please feel free at this point to utter your favourite Anglo-Saxon expletive here in a very loud voice. But do note that we're not out to rubbish what may be perfectly real cases of reincarnation, which have manifested without the need of hypnosis. They do seem to exist, though without the opportunity to have them tested in a rigorous way it's impossible to say with any certainty how real they may be. Unfortunately, again attesting to the power of suggestion, nearly all cases are found in countries where a large section of the populace has a religious reason for believing in reincarnation.

'Real' hypnosis?

Ian: "I became very interested in hypnotism at an early age and, as a teenager, spent many happy summer nights for about 4 years watching a wonderful hypnotist called Joseph Karma perform for the seaside crowds where I lived. I soon became a regular volunteer for his shows, not just because of my interest in hypnosis, but also because (mercenary as it sounds!) every volunteer got trinkets and tickets to further performances, so it was a handy incentive to make my friends and I show up when we could. The best volunteers each evening would be asked to appear in a Friday show that featured only the top subjects from previous shows. Appearing in this performance meant being given even bigger rewards for our help, including a couple of bottles of beer. As a way of getting compliant, entertaining subjects on stage this was a phenomenal success, and the Friday show was always hilarious. But the point is that I was shy and very introverted at this time in my life. Even so, I realised that when I was on stage I could act however I wanted to, as long as that excuse of 'being hypnotised' was supporting me.

As I was of course very interested to see who was and wasn't hypnotised with me on those nights I made it on stage, I talked to quite a few of the other volunteers about their experience. I can only remember a few who seemed truly befuddled and confused about what had gone on, the rest of us agreeing to an unspoken 'honour amongst thieves', keeping what had truly happened to ourselves rather than tell our waiting friends the truth."

Is stage hypnosis a sham then? Not at all. It works on those it works on. Given more time than stage shows allow for the hypnotist to attend closely to every individual subject, its success rate in creating extreme suggestibility would be very high, possibly 80% and more. Without the luxury of masses of time, as long as people act as they should it doesn't matter who is hypnotised and who isn't. Really the show's the thing, and anyone who will contribute to it convincingly and in an entertaining way - hypnotised or not - helps deepen the illusion for the audience and for the other volunteers who *are* buying it.

How then do people - some of them normally very introvert - eat lemons as though they were sweet apples, or dance with fairies, or sing show tunes (badly!) in front of people they don't know? The fact that they don't know the rest of the audience helps rather than hinders, but really, pretending to be hypnotised is in some ways like being drunk. You have a reason to act out of character, to step freely outside the bounds of the behaviour that people normally expect from you. Being able to be demonstrative and act up for an audience with no worries about getting it right or wrong, to be the centre of attention, is very liberating and will cause most subjects to rise to the occasion. People will often ask volunteers afterwards, "How could you do those things on stage and not know you were doing them?" No matter what the volunteer says, the real reasons will tend to be: because they had an excuse; because they can say that they don't remember what they did and nobody can prove otherwise; because they now have a good story to tell; or even because they really *were* hypnotised.

For obvious reasons it's rare that you'll hear a hypnotist talk about the pitfalls of hypnosis, or the fact that it isn't able to do all the remarkable things it's supposed to. Even in some instructional books the authors will still try to keep all the myths that surround it going, as the more powerful the subject and public assume hypnosis to be the greater the effect it has on them.

All we'd like you to do is to be careful not to be fooled by the image that hypnosis has - but fool *with* it.

Medical Hypnosis

Medical hypnosis, as opposed to stage hypnosis, is a slightly different creature to the kind of 'Waking Hypnosis' we're going to use here. Although it's not really necessary to understand the difference between 'waking' and 'medical' hypnosis, we think it will help to talk a little about what both are so that you can understand the basis of them more fully.

A medical hypnotist will usually use suggestion to create deep relaxation in the subject, then help them to create an imaginary setting, a 'safe place' in which the therapy will take place. Once secure and fully relaxed, the hypnotist can then turn what would normally be the patient's random ideas into guided imagery, creating situations where he can help them tackle phobias and obsessions.

In medical hypnosis they tend to refer to the hypnotic state as being 'hypnogogic' or 'hypnopompic' - a condition where you're not quite awake, but not asleep either. You pass through this same state twice each day for up to a few minutes at a time: once when you're waking up and once when you go to sleep. If you've ever had an experience where someone has come into your bedroom and talked to you or done something that you later have no recollection of, even though at the time you appeared to be wide awake and rational, that's the 'hypnogogic /hypnopompic' state. A point where the subject is approaching/leaving sleep and experiencing random dream-like thoughts - and perhaps also experiencing *real* events as dreams - without actually being asleep.

Waking Hypnosis

Stage hypnosis - 'Waking Hypnosis' - employs different, speedier methods to create extreme suggestibility. In essence, stage hypnosis creates and exploits self-doubt, suggestions and inferences, piling strange effect on effect until the subject is left with no other choice but to believe that what the performer is telling them is true. When a strange event occurs at the hands of a mentalist or hypnotist that the subject has no explanation for, they will, at the very least, begin to doubt the accuracy of their perceptions. Creating doubt about a volunteer's ability to judge the reality of any event is a major part of building ongoing suggestibility in them. If they can't explain the first strange occurrence you subject them to they'll be more likely to accept the next one out of hand - they have become 'suggestible'.

As a very simple example of suggestion, try this. Take a transparent plastic carton of skimmed milk and pour natural cottage cheese into it until it looks lumpy. If you can later stomach it, pour a few drops of oil into the container too (we suggest using groundnut oil for this as it doesn't have any kind of fatty taste to it). Now, what you've just made up is a pretty good visual simulacra of carton of very sour milk. A watery medium containing fatty lumps and yellow-ish oil that would fool most people, even on close inspection.

At any gathering of people, open the carton and take a sniff of the contents, wrinkling your nose and jerking your head back as though you've just experienced the worst smell ever. Comment on it loudly, as you would if it were really sour, making sure that everyone around you knows what's happening. You might even swallow hard a couple of times too as though you're holding back nausea, rubbing at your solar plexus to calm your queasy stomach. As a piece of handling, thrust the carton under the noses of those who seem to believe you the most, asking them to take a good sniff and see what they think. Many will run a mile, but most of those who *do* dare to take the carton will not want to smell what you're offering and will just pretend that they're sniffing it instead - but will still act disgusted in just the way that you have. To everyone else this is proof that the milk is really sour.

Now say that you're going to drink it anyway. Pour the contents into a glass, allowing a little time for the cheese lumps to become very visible to the spectators and the oil to rise to the top of the glass, then down it with gusto! Let some dribble down your chin, even gag slightly as you drink the first mouthfuls. The more acting you can put into this performance the greater (and we guarantee, the more pleasing!) the effect will be.

This works incredibly well because it piles a series of suggestions one on top of the other about how bad the milk really is. Your reaction to the milk as you first opened the carton; the visible lumps and oil; the non-existent smell that many people will react to, reinforcing the illusion for those who have not. Most spectators present will now have been fooled by visual, emotional and imagined olfactory cues all at once, causing them to believe at face value the idea that the milk is truly repugnant. Trick one sense and you *might* fool a spectator, trick two or three senses and they'll believe anything.

The Problem of Recovered Memories

By being open about how some hypnotic effects work we don't want it to sound as though we're being dismissive of hypnosis as a whole. Correctly delivered suggestion is immeasurably powerful and is used so extensively and effectively by advertising, governments and general media that we're responding to it every day without even realising it. Used carefully it can even give us memories of things that have never happened.

The use of photographs by psychotherapists as memory cues for the 'recovery' of patients' possible past trauma has been called into question by a recent Canadian study. When subjects were given suggestions (which were supplemented with a class photo) that they had taken part in a fictitious childhood event, researchers found that a 'staggering' two-out-of-three subjects used in the test accepted the event as having really happened to them.

"I was flabbergasted to have attained such an exceptionally high rate of quite elaborate false memory reports," said University of Victoria psychology professor, Dr. Stephen Lindsay (Psychological Science, March 2004).

Forty-five first year psychology students were told three stories about their grade-school experiences and asked about their memories of them. Two of the accounts were of real grade three to six events, told to the researchers by the participant's parents. The third event was fictitious, but also attributed to the parents, and related how the subject and a friend got into trouble for playing a prank on a schoolteacher.

The subjects were encouraged to recall the prank through a combination of guided imagery and 'mental context re-instatement - basically imagining they were back in grade school. Half of the participants were also given their real grade-one class photograph to supplement the guided imagery, which had a surprising effect on their belief in the false event.

About a quarter of the participants without a photo' said they had some memory of it; but a phenomenal 67% of those with a photo' claimed to have an actual, "richly detailed", memory of the non-event.

"The findings support the general theoretical perspective that memories aren't things that are stored somewhere in your head," says Professor Lindsay. "Memories are experiences that we can have that arise through an interaction between things that really have happened to us in the past and our current expectations and beliefs."

In the 1980's,'recovering' repressed childhood trauma memories was encouraged by such popular books as, 'The Courage to Heal'. Although less popular now, some psychotherapists still use suggestive memory 'recovery' techniques like those above.

"Our results argue for caution in the use of any of these suggestive techniques," said Dr. Lindsay. "Results like these support the concern that they increase the likelihood that people will experience false memories."

Complex as our minds may be, they're still wide open to manipulation and error.

9

The Analysis Machine

Let's take a brief rest from looking at suggestion and examine an intriguing effect that, although it's been known of for at least a century, has hardly been explored at all by science. We feel that it's only a matter of time before somebody produces a mentalist routine that makes use of this baffling experiment - and who knows, that somebody could be you. Basically what we have here is an analysis 'machine' that makes use of natural body processes and inherent human abilities to help you literally feel the difference between one type of object and another at an almost molecular level.

We've found that it works best at first if the objects tested have a radically different physical makeup. But in fact after a little use you'll be able to use it to tell the difference between a sound limb and an unwell one, or a piece of fresh fish from one that's a mere two days old. Why this hasn't been made more use of we're unsure, but the potential for use in mentalism is obviously stunning.

EXPERIMENT 1

You'll need:
- Any citrus fruit (orange, lemon, etc)
- Any small but fairly solid inanimate object, such as a book, bottle or pen.
- A piece of flat glass. Window glass, a mirror or picture glass is perfect for this. Thickness doesn't matter, but try to avoid anti-reflective or smoked glass as it reduces the depth of effect.

Method
Sit at a table with the glass laying flat in front of you. Using preferably the index finger of your right hand, stroke the glass gently a few times to gain a sense of how it feels to the touch when it's 'neutral'.

Try to get used to stroking the glass in exactly the same way each time. Focus is important here, don't do this half-heartedly as the sensations are very subtle at first - and, just as importantly, try to stay very relaxed.

After establishing your control sensations, accustoming yourself to the feeling of the glass, take the citrus fruit in your left hand, relax, and begin to stroke the glass plate again. Does it now feel slicker, more adhesive, or perhaps smoother - or as some users say 'runnier'?

Now put down the fruit and take up the inanimate object and do the same thing. You should notice immediately that the glass feels completely different depending on what type of object you're holding. Although not everyone can feel a totally radical change in sensation, almost everyone finds the difference quite noticeable after the first couple of attempts.

EXPERIMENT 2

For this one you need:
- Two cartons of milk, one at least 2 days older than the other.
- The services of a volunteer. For some reason women are better at this than men, but in general terms the effect should stay pretty much the same no matter what the sex of the subject you choose.

Method

The volunteer is asked to hold her left arm out sideways from her body, palm down, at about shoulder height. You stand in front of and a little to the side of her, placing your left hand on her left shoulder and your right hand on the back of her left wrist. You then push down on the wrist with the subject resisting your pressure until the arm finally gives way. When it does, try to evaluate just how hard you had to push and how hard they had to resist to make this happen. Again this is your control test, so it's very important that you eventually learn to recognise it as a neutral state.

Allow the subject to lower their arm to rest it for a minute or so before continuing.

Now give her the fresher of the two milk cartons to hold in her right hand and do the experiment again, in particular looking for any changes in your volunteer's ability to resist your pressure.

Finally, have your subject take up the older milk carton and repeat the process, again noting the required pressure and resistance. The difference between the two cartons should be quite pronounced and you may find that the subject find resisting your downwards pressure almost impossible as she holds the least fresh milk carton!

Both experiments have a million applications, from finding fresh food and water to helping you assess any food sensitivities and allergies your subjects might have. Try both experiments regularly on as many substances as you can to help build up your sensing skills.

10

Suggestion & the Subject

Before we go on with our exploration of suggestion and move more deeply into hypnosis, it's important to understand that the subject's perception of you plays a major role in how effective your suggestions are on them. If you show just the right combination of friendliness and authority people will be eager to comply with what you ask them to do. But get the mix wrong and very little will work at all.

Image, Challenge and Respect

Let's be honest about one aspect of mentalism; much of what's done and said is to create a mysterious air around the performer to help insinuate that he or she has powers that others don't. Apart from the image this helps create, once this idea of greater ability is established in the subject, the more likely any routines you do will work on them. If a volunteer believes you really can do what you say you can then they'll also be far less likely to look for trickery and just get on with experiencing what you're doing to or with them.

But many stage performers try to build on this idea of dominance, mystery and authority to the point where it works to their own detriment. Whether you're walking on stage or walking up to someone in the street, who you seem to be in that first moment of contact makes the difference between a successful and entertaining performance and a total disaster. Being too dominant or mysterious is just as bad as being too ordinary and having no charisma.

Imagine you're the average spectator, neither a believer nor non-believer. A man walks on stage all dressed in black, makes theatrical gestures and talks about 'dark powers' that he can wield over his subjects. A high percentage of people in the audience will immediately be challenged by this performer; his blatant idea that he could hold any sway over them and his references to abilities that they don't believe in.

Even his clothes and script smack of manipulative staging and image building. They hate him before he's even begun his act and he'll need to work very hard to restore himself to validity in their eyes.

In some cases, as some notable performers have learned to their cost, their acceptance as mentalists/hypnotists may literally depend on the country they're playing in. What works well in America for example as a marvellous display of a deep and dangerous character performing minor miracles, can tend to be thought of as laughable and pretentious in England.

But worst of all, the 'darker' the persona you try to create the less it allows you to backtrack and mould who you're pretending to be to the needs and expectations of the audience. If you have a very rigid 'dark' stage image you can't allow power sharing and subtle negotiation with disruptive spectators because that would be seen as weakening your authority. You also can't be seen to laugh nor act as a normal, fallible human being when you need to either, which is paramount to the success of some routines. If you decide on one particular persona for your stage performance you can be stuck with it - and not be able to use psychological ploys to get yourself out of awkward situations that would be seen as out of character with the way your audience has perceived you. Although it seems counter intuitive to the whole mentalist ethos, there'll be lots of occasions when you need to be seen as less dominant, less weird and downright normal if you're going to succeed.

Don't establish your credentials at every opportunity and say 'I am this'. Let your audience make up their own minds about who you are and what you can do. Let your image grow from your act, mould who you need to be for one particular subject, or one particular audience as their expectations dictate. Don't trap yourself in a 'set in stone' character.

The Good Subject

It would be nice if we were all on television and every time we asked for a volunteer they (and the audience) acted as we want them to. In theatres, audiences bind themselves as a whole to being more co-operative and pleasant than they would for impromptu performers where the mood of the spectators can be rowdy and controlled by just one or two people. Understanding the psychology of your subjects and audience in these situations is of course important for any mentalist, helping you understand whether or not a particular suggestion routine will work on a subject and why.

In terms of your participants, we'd just like to talk briefly about the types of subject you might come across. If you're asking for volunteers rather than just going up to people in the street and pressing them into taking part in what you do, you need to be very aware of why they might want to agree.

In the average Hypnosis show you might use induction tests (like those in the next chapter) to cull 14 volunteers down to 5 or 6 really good subjects. But in Mentalism you might only get one volunteer that you have to work with no matter what. Nobody can provide hard and fast rules about how any person you choose will act as you work with them, but if you have a basic understanding about why each volunteer *may* be there it will help prepare you for at least the main eventualities. People may volunteer:

- To experience - to have a good time and perhaps take part in something that will enthral them and that they can tell friends and family about
- To entertain - to perform for the audience as much as you will.
- To destroy - to be the nightmare subject, trying to sabotage your routine.

Of course, the first two are perfect subjects. It doesn't matter to them whether the trick works or not, they'll *always* say that it has. Even if an effect visibly and painfully fails on them, their entertaining antics will usually make up for it. But the third...well, usually they'll see themselves as 'The Judge', there to see that fair play is carried out on behalf of everyone else. They're happy, eager and co-operative, but they're also there to get a closer look at what you're doing, just in case. Don't mistake anyone's eagerness to take part in what you're doing for a belief in it. Many of those first up on stage will be there to test you out.

They may not be actively obstructive, but if they're watching you closely they can ask awkward questions at awkward times.

However, not all nightmare subjects are demon spawn who take evil pleasure in your failure. Sometimes a subject's expectations of hypnosis and Mentalism are so high that they're scared of what may occur and wont allow themselves to take part co-operatively in a routine - even if they've already offered their services and are sitting ready for action in front of you. Despite having enough confidence to volunteer in the first place they can't get over their subconscious terror of giving up control to you. This is common in seemingly out-going types who show an extrovert manner to hide the fact that in reality they feel inferior to others and believe that if they were to fully succumb to you they'd be easy meat and might end up making a fool of themselves. When they do co-operate they'll do as you ask only to a limited extent and will seem to constantly misinterpret your directions as the routine progresses. This isn't bloody minded-ness, just fear that you might embarrass them, or ruin their image of intelligence and leadership by showing that they too can be taken in as any 'lesser' person might. They don't want to be seen to be obstructive, but they just can't allow themselves to be seen to have been duped by you and will resort to whatever means they can to make sure that it never takes place.

Go on then, hypnotise me...

Although in hypnosis you would normally steer clear of any participant who begins by saying something like, "I'll bet you can't hypnotise me!", if you have the time to allay the fears of this type of person they can be interesting to work on. Usually they'll see themselves as the most powerful within the group, or the most outgoing and they'll therefore have the unspoken respect of many of the other volunteers or audience. But their statement can indicate a real fear in them that you might actually be able to gain some kind of control over them, that they fear their own weakness. If this is the case, they may respond well as a subject because of their fear. If you can be seen to make even them respond to an effect positively you've gone a long way to establish your abilities to everyone present.

If you can't use a disruptive subject or get them 'off-stage', use this person to aid and abet yourself whenever possible. If you ask them to help you they tend to feel that what you're saying is, "I know I can't fool you with this stuff, how about we both work together?", which appeals to their egos no end.

Rather than trying to dominate them, giving them an outright reason to fight back, talk to them like they're equal in this 'experiment', *because* of their objectivity and cynicism. Tell them, yes, they're right, there's no way that anyone who doesn't want to be hypnotised (or whatever it is you're purporting to do) can ever be 'put under' and made to do anything which they would not normally do when 'awake', which is true. Also explain that this isn't a battle of wills, with one side trying to outwit the other, but a co-operative experiment. By saying this you remove the challenge to them, the idea that if they do become hypnotised you have 'beaten' them. You might also say that people like them tend to make the best subjects of all, if they allow themselves to be, because they won't exaggerate whatever occurs or play up to the audience. Finish by openly admitting you can't work with them, "I do of course understand that this kind of thing isn't for you, so I'll use someone else..."

Having said all of this you can now leave 'Mr Disruptive' to mull things over for a little while, and go back working with more responsive subjects instead. He'll usually eventually see that these volunteers are having much more fun than he is and are at the centre of fun and attention. As this place is usually reserved for him, he'll now tend to want to get involved in what's happening again. Give him a sincere chance to get back into the act. Don't include him begrudgingly or you still have an enemy who may try to disrupt things; welcome him back gratefully, as though he can now help you take the performance to greater heights.

To help guard against conflicts like those above, when using any form of hypnotic suggestion it's best to define the ideal subject to the audience as soon as possible before you've picked your volunteers. Say that a good subject is usually intelligent, imaginative and brave enough to allow whatever happens to happen. Once you've done this, if anyone then counters with, "You can't hypnotise me", it's like they're saying that they're not any of these things.

There are of course ten of reasons why someone might want to volunteer their services, but on the whole the small selection we list here and their variations are amongst the most common. If you're doing impromptu effects on the spot, choosing a subject out of a sea (or small pool) of faces can be a daunting task until you learn to recognise those who want to participate just for fun and with no hidden agenda.

Ian: "From a purely hypnosis point of view I tend to use people who have to be coaxed into participating rather than those who leap forward at the first opportunity. Confident people are more likely to be able to openly voice their doubts about what you're doing and are more likely to be the nightmare subject we all dread. Not in every case obviously, but it's better to aim for the quieter members of your audience who might feel slightly awed or even intimidated by the proceedings. Their fear can amplify the effect of anything that may happen to them to a large degree. I don't mean it to sound harsh, but I'd certainly tend to go for those weaker members of the group rather than the most outgoing."

Martin; "In mentalism it's obviously also preferable - if you're using methods where the subject should, for example, choose a number that the majority of people would choose - that your subjects are going to act like 'the majority'. Whether they do or not rests on their character (and yours), the level of rapport you've reached and how much they want you to succeed. It can't be an exact science to say that this or that kind of person will do what you expect of them and sometimes you can only tell how someone's going to react by actually doing a routine with them."

Belief, Fluidity and Expectation

These are things that give vast power to any routine and increase the effectiveness of suggestion on your subjects ten-fold. It doesn't matter if you're trying to hypnotise someone or doing a mentalist effect on them, these are the main things that will affect the outcome.

Ian: "Let me just illustrate how important fluidity and expectation can be. Comparing the format of each of Karma's shows I visited, the first thing I realised was that what he did wasn't static, he moulded each performance not only to the audience, but of course also to the suggestibility of his subjects. Although there were many things that stayed the same in each show, on the whole it was very necessary for him to base his pacing and routines on how entertaining his subjects were being. This is true for any hypnotist or mentalist. A performance can't be a fixed thing that you adhere rigidly to, you're just creating a situation for yourself whereby if anything goes wrong you have no way of getting back on track. But, if your performance is fluid, every reaction - good and bad - is expected and can be responded to. If what you're doing isn't entertaining your audience you need the skill and capacity to be able to move on into something else that might please them more. You may call yourself a magician, a hypnotist or a mentalist; but you must remember above all that first and foremost you're an entertainer. Make entertaining - not image building - your priority.

Conversely, if something goes particularly right in your act you need just as much space and time on stage to exploit it as when things go wrong. One event in a show Karma did was a perfect example of fluid performance and maximising a situation.

It was a normal night, with a dozen or so volunteers filing up on stage, each one in turn tested for susceptibility to suggestion then seated if they were suitable. Everything up until this point had been a standard format show, until Karma came to one particular girl who stood back nervously until all of the 'friends' who had hauled her up against her wishes had been through the process of induction.

She was about 18 years old and Irish, one of the many seasonal workers who were employed by the hotels in the town. She stood wringing her hands as Karma's eyes fell on her. They both stood in silence for a very long time as he fixed her with his gaze, adding to her anguish. Then he nodded and his assistant brought the girl to him at the front of the stage. Nothing was said for long seconds, probably seeming like hours to the girl. Now even more nervous she looked to her friends and then the audience for some support, but still Karma didn't speak. Then, just as she turned her head back to shyly look up at him, Karma suddenly pointed to his left eye and shouted, "Sleep!" - and the girl fell unconscious into the arms of his assistant.

Expectation.

This girl had no idea what hypnosis was, how it felt or how it was carried out; but when Karma issued this command to 'Sleep!', something deep inside her brain said, *"THIS* is it." And she slept.

Karma had seen his opportunity and demonstrated a very old principle that's been used by countless hypnotists over the years. Here was a nervous, suggestible girl who would create her own version of an hypnotic trance based purely on her expectation of what a real trance would be. All she needed was a trigger, some event or movement by the hypnotist that would signal when she should 'sleep'. All he had to do was time it correctly, with a long enough build up to increase her trepidation - and best of all, fear - and with the right trigger she would place herself in an unconscious state.

Taken to sit (still unconscious) on a chair at the side of the stage the girl wasn't up to taking part in the rest of the performance, but as you can imagine, just having her sitting there as proof of Karma's 'power' had a remarkably positive effect on his audience! He moulded the rest of the evening around returning to the girl and describing the depth of her trance, making sure that nobody forgot how simply he had placed her into this state. Without a fluid approach to his own act, there would have been little time to take advantage of the situation that her arrival on stage presented."

Hypnotic stage acts, particularly during the 20's and 30's used exactly the same effect, usually at the moment that a volunteer was being helped up onto the stage. A sudden shout into their faces, even a slap or sudden twist of their heads was all it took for them to decide, just as the girl above did, that *this* was Hypnosis."

As we said earlier, whether they were really hypnotised or not doesn't matter. As far as the audience were concerned the subjects had entered a hypnotic state at that moment and were acting accordingly. Also, whether the subjects themselves were or weren't hypnotised didn't matter to them either. They now had an excuse to act in exactly the way they were told to. As a mentalist, what your audience and subjects expect is just as important as what you actually give them.

Ian: "I was about 9 years old when I got my first lesson in psychology and expectation from my primary school teacher, Mrs Gittens. As it was a very small school where on occasion there were hardly enough children to hold a lesson with, Mrs Gittens would sometimes tell us stories about things that interested her to fill the time. Even now I remember noting how intrigued she herself seemed with what she was telling us and how much more she seemed to want to say about it. But, as none of us were over the age of 10 I'm sure she didn't want to do more than hint at the possibilities of it all, or risk having us going out into the world playing happily (and probably very destructively!) with other people's minds.

She told us two stories, both of which have stayed with me ever since and totally changed how I viewed other people. In the first one she spoke of an experiment carried out in a laboratory just before World War 2 by scientists trying to find out just how much belief played a part in our view of reality. A subject was told that the scientists were trying to evaluate pain tolerance in adults, looking for ways to minimise it in preparation for the coming war. A bar of red hot iron was to be placed against the subject's leg until he couldn't take the pain anymore, giving them a rough idea of each individual's level of tolerance.

With a lot of medical preparation of the area where the iron was to be applied and doctors standing by in case of mishaps, the subject was then blindfolded and strapped into a chair to stop involuntary movements away from the hot iron. In the same way that any Mentalist might today, the subject was given chances to back out of the experiment, telling them that what they were about to go through could well be agony. Eventually the iron is pressed to the subject's calf and he screams out, almost fainting with the pain. After he signals that he can take it no longer the iron is removed and his leg is quickly bandaged to 'reduce the chances of infection'.

Looking at the wound the following day the scientists find a deep burn and blistering on the subject's leg, which takes a further month to heal. What's remarkable about this is the fact that the iron was actually icy cold, not red hot. All it took was a little build up and lots of expectation on the subject's part and his body mechanisms leapt into action to help repair a burn that never was.

The second story, though simpler, was just as valuable a lesson and centred around the obvious but often ignored fact that our external and internal realities are only what we believe them to be.

Something of a tearaway at her own school as a child, Mrs Gittens and some friends chose an unpopular girl as their 'victim' and one by one throughout the day simply told her how ill she looked. By the end of the afternoon the girl was ill enough to be sent home to her parents with a debilitating (but unknown) illness that was giving her headaches, nausea and vomiting.

As you can imagine, this was wonderful stuff to me as a fascinated 9 year old. The power of suggestion, the power of belief. By the time I was 12 I'd read most of the books on hypnosis I could find and was practising whenever I could on the few people who would let me. My success was mixed of course, having absolutely zero authority to wield other than over one or two class rejects who were lower in the school pecking order than I was, though who responded very well. But this was all good training that allowed me to understand various aspects of Hypnosis at a quite early age.

A few years later a friend and I were trying to hypnotise a girl from our village who was, even at that age, very cynical. I'd taken her through all the basic induction techniques and got what I thought were reasonable results, with the girl, Sarah, now lying in a suggestible state on our couch. But now she was there and supposedly 'hypnotised', what could we do next? I had her believe her hands were very light and floating, then so heavy she couldn't lift them, etc - but it all seemed just a bit dull and we couldn't really be sure if she was play-acting or not.

Then my friend suggested that we should try to anaesthetise her hand and see if we could stick pins in it. Not a bad idea I agreed, a good experiment *and* a test of whether she was hypnotised or not. After a long sequence of suggestion I lifted the skin on the back of her hand whilst my friend gleefully (a bit too gleefully now I come to think of it!) pushed a darning needle all the way through it. To both our pleasure, not a flinch, not a glimmer of reaction appeared on her face.

The needle was then passed again through a thicker flap of skin with the same result. Then my friend even more gleefully scratched a large 'S' into her skin that immediately came up in a blood oozing weal. Still no response. This was a major result for me, my first real, provable experience of someone becoming deeply open to suggestion - or so I thought.

After a little more fooling around I woke her up with a reverse count, eager to know what the 'trance' had felt like. I'm paraphrasing a lot here, but put in a nutshell she opened her eyes and laughed in our faces, saying, "Haha, suckers! I was acting all along!"

Well, she'd got us we agreed sheepishly. But how on earth had she managed to stay still while we put the needle through her hand, we asked? Sarah looked at her hand and paled significantly, bordering on fainting and vomiting. She had no idea that we'd even touched her hand, let alone pushed a needle through it.

Though that was the last time she let me practise on her (I've never been sure why...), Sarah had taught me a wonderful lesson about hypnosis. Playing the game with the hypnotist, even with the aim of fooling him and any spectators, makes you very focussed on responding as he or she wants you to. Putting your heart and soul into the deception can actually make your very open to suggestion. At what point does pretending to be hypnotised turn into actually being hypnotised?"

Respect

Imagine you're in your kitchen at home, having a conversation with your favourite movie star/scientist/writer - anyone you like and respect.

As you talk they reach into your refrigerator and take out a soft-drink can - but as they take it out of the cooler they drop the can to the ground and yell out, "That's red hot!"

What would you think?

Ian: "Personally - and I have to say that this is truthful, despite me knowing what I know - I would think that maybe somebody had placed a hot can in the cooler. Or perhaps there was a malfunction that had caused the can to heat up. The more I liked and respected the person the less likely I would be to think the obvious - simply that they were lying."

This teaches us a lot about who and how much we're prepared to believe if the circumstances are right. Belief, in terms of believing what anyone else tells you, is based almost solely on respect.

This brings us back to the theme of persona again, as you'll have noticed *two* important words in the above: 'liked' and 'respected', and it's important that you try to be both. You might feel that as long as your routines work and are well presented you're fine. But if there's no liking there then it's still an uphill struggle to get the audience to actually enjoy what you're presenting to them. If you're liked, your subjects want your routines to work and, more importantly, there are fewer problems with domination and challenge to overcome.

If someone you respect makes an outlandish statement then at the very least you're going to have doubts about any conflicting evidence your senses may be telling you. You're completely prepared to withhold a normal world-view based on the words or actions of another simply because you respect them.

Confidence

Supposing you were a mentalist subject on stage in front of 500 people, all of whom you imagine to be watching the proceedings very closely. The mentalist says to you, "...And now you'll see your hands turn slowly into the branches of a tree, extending outwards and growing leaves..."

No matter how loudly your brain yells, "That's not possible!", another part of your brain is going to be analysing the situation and thinking, "How can he say such a thing in front of all these people if it's not true?" That doubt in the subject's logic is sometimes all it takes to draw them into a very suggestible state.

Although it can be a dangerous tack to take if you don't have the skills to back it up, being bold in your presentations will establish the idea in your subject's minds that you are able to do the impossible. *With the right subject* you can take any of the suggestibility tests/induction methods that follow and do them without any suggestion other than stating bluntly that they WILL happen as you have described beforehand.

In the later 'Arm Raising' induction for example it's usual to continue with subtle vocal and physical suggestion until the subject's arm is raised off a table. But if you had the confidence, had good rapport and created a sense of some authority over your subject, you could alternatively simply state at the beginning of the effect that over the next few minutes they will feel their arm getting lighter and lighter until it rises up into the air. Then you stand by the subject's side (or look them intently in the eyes) in complete silence as you wait for the effect to take place. Whether it would work or not is down to the relationship between you and your volunteer, but on the whole this approach would work on a high proportion of people.

The power of this period of silence lies in casting doubt on the subject's own opinion of what is and isn't possible. You've made this statement that his or her arm will rise up in front of 'X' amount of people and now appear so confident that it will happen that you're just standing waiting. To any logical thinker that makes them doubt what years of experience has told them simply can not take place. It might be a small doubt, but it'll be just big enough to make them watch their own arm and wonder, is this really going to happen? Is it happening now? Was that little twitch my hand just made the start of it?

A confident statement, no matter how strange, can have a massive effect on both your subjects and your audience. But as we've said, this is a dangerous ploy if you're using it with routines that don't have a guaranteed effect. All it takes is for one thing you've confidently asserted will take place not to happen and your image is dented for the rest of the performance. Or is it? If you actually build the possibility of failure into your effects - have the audience almost expect it, and on your say so - then you're giving yourself an escape route and a handy affirmation that what you do *is* working on a very strange mental level.

How?

Failure

Establishing the possibility of failure into a mentalist routine is a way of saying that what you're able to do isn't just a simple trick, done using a set of props and therefore infallible. In the later routines we describe, the 'Chi effect' is used as a get out for the performer and the subject. If something doesn't work then it's because the performer wasn't tuned in to the Chi properly, or even better, that perhaps the subject was a little nervous and not able to concentrate enough to manifest it. You might want to attribute everything you do to an unnamed power instead, or to 'ideomotor responses'; if so just change the example wording that follows to something that you're more comfortable with and that fits better into the style of your own act. As with all scripting you have to make sure that what you say sounds like it's in your own words.

During your opening patter for such effects you might say something like, "I don't know if this is going to work, it really depends on the subject and a lot of other factors. But I think you should be a good person to try this out on..." In one statement you've removed the idea that you're challenging the subject (who might not like your persona) to fight back and stop the routine from working. You're also putting a lot of the success of the effect down to powers outside of your control - and to the abilities of your participant. You've also taken your routines beyond being 'normal' magic, because normal magic *always* works as far as your audience is concerned. Anyone who is prepared to get up on stage and say that odd things only MAY happen must be using methods that don't rely on props that would ensure they certainly WOULD happen.

Luck, chance & opportunity

Martin: "I was invited to a wine-tasting party at my friend James house few months ago. As usual there was much more swallowing than tasting being done and eventually James waggled an accusing finger at me and said to everybody, "Martin here does this...thing. " This is his way of saying, "Go on, do something weird for us...", which of course I happily did, as the least I could offer in return for having been served some excellent wines and French cheeses all night. On top of that my job is always a bit easier if people have had just a little to drink (not too much though), as they tend to let their barriers down after the first glass or two. So, I did a few effects: a bit of mind-reading, a spooky story effect where people from beyond the grave suddenly interrupt the party, with wineglasses falling over and so forth. I had a good time and it seemed everybody else was having one too.

I should point out that James doesn't really understand what it is I do. I've never stated psychic powers (nor would I), but he asked me once if I did actually possess them and could see and do things that normal people couldn't. I gave him the 'standard' mentalist explanation I always use, that I, "...use my five senses and NLP and hypnotic techniques to create the illusion of a sixth sense." Over time, in James' world this has become simply, 'Martin's thing'. In reality I think he's still very confused, but he always enjoys my party tricks so I haven't felt the need to explain myself further so far.

Anyway, having done a few impromptu routines we eventually got back to the mandatory grading of the wines, which happily involved even more 'tasting'. Being the host James went first and did *his* thing, frowning and gargling his way through various vintages as he mentally rated them, saying nothing about how he scored each. Then it was my turn and he watched me carefully as I sampled his latest acquisitions and announced my numerical quality grading, one by one.

Now, I really wish I could say that I'd planned what was to come, but unfortunately I can't. As I gave my verdict on each wine, James's jaw dropped further and further. When I was done his eyes narrowed. "How the HELL did you do that?", he said. Although inside I was thinking, "Uuuuh?", I managed to keep a poker face, not quite sure exactly what it was I was meant to have done.

"Did you read it in my face? My eyes...?", he went on. "How *did* you do it?" And that was when it hit me - I had rated the wines exactly the same as James had.

A complete coincidence of course, or the same taste in wine one could argue, but I took the opportunity and played along, thus gaining a whole bag of Brownie points for myself without the need of actually working for them. To this day (and until James or one of the other guests read this book) everybody at the party thinks that I'm capable of divining people's deepest thoughts by, as I told them, 'reading facial muscle movements.' A load of BS, obviously, but it was the first thing that popped into my head at the time. I must have delivered it in a fairly convincing way, as everyone present nodded and seemed to go, "Uh...okay," as though it was the most natural explanation possible. Nobody took me to task over it and the only questions I was asked afterwards were all about how and where this amazing tool could be learned.

In their eyes this was perhaps one of the best and certainly most talked about 'effects' of the evening - and it came out of nowhere.

The morale of this story (apart from the obvious, that one should always accept an invitation to a wine tasting) is that every once in a while a possibility will present itself out of the blue. Be ready to grab it when it does arrive and the chances are you'll get results beyond your wildest dreams.

11

Hypnotic Inductions

The first couple of methods here ('Inductions') use a combination of suggestion and a physical effect to create powerful illusions. Beyond that we're going to take a look at methods that rely completely on suggestion. Once you've understood the following preliminaries and have had a chance to practise them, using pure suggestion will then become much easier to implement.

There are quite a few simple techniques that'll help you establish a state of suggestibility in your subjects. The following three routines are all based on well-known methods - which are both tests of susceptibility to suggestion and also ways of bringing about a more suggestible state. The wonderful thing about induction 'tests' is that you can easily incorporate them into a performance as they can be very entertaining to watch.

As with any of the best induction methods these effects don't just rely on how suggestible your subject is but, as we say above, also on a real physical effect too. Regardless of whether the participant buys into the suggestion part of the routine, none will be able to deny the physical aspects of what they're experiencing.

It really doesn't matter if any induction technique you use doesn't work on every subject, that isn't the point of doing them. The idea is to use them to help you decide exactly which one of your volunteers will respond as you need them to. If an induction doesn't work on Mr 'A', but does on Mr 'B' then obviously you might thank 'A' for his efforts and return him to the audience.

Usually in stage hypnosis the hypnotist will have his or her own way of moving a volunteer from the induction test into a 'real' hypnotic state - sometimes with a sudden movement of the subject's head, perhaps pressing it forward and down on their chest while saying, "Sleep", etc. But do the subjects really go into any kind of hypnotic condition at that point? As we said previously, on two opposite ends of the scale, those with high expectancy and openness to suggestion will, those who aren't listening or are purposely playacting and getting away with it won't. There's also a whole range of other subject types in between these two extremes who may or may not become 'hypnotised'.

The physical method used to hypnotise (or not), such as pressing down on the subject's head, is both a signal to the subject and a signal to the audience too. It says to them that from this point on this person is hypnotised, expect different behaviour from them. And the subject will also act differently, because he too has recognised the signal for the 'trance' to begin. He now knows that he can do things he would never have dared, and without judgement, because he's now 'hypnotised' and can say hand on heart for the rest of his life that he was 'out' and has no memory of what happened.

For a lot of people the signal *will* trigger a real state of...something. But, there's nothing to say that two people who have responded well to suggestion and are now 'hypnotised' (whatever that truly means) are in the exact same mindset at all. Both subjects may look and act the exactly same. When it comes down to it, how much of a difference is there between the two and, for the sake of performance, does it matter?

Although subjects may well show all the same symptoms, such as an almost instant positive response to your commands, there's nothing to say that each person isn't creating an entirely different state for himself or herself. As most will have only a scant knowledge of hypnotic 'trance' that will tend to be based more on folklore than reality, many will self-create a condition that makes them even more responsive to suggestion than someone who is in a real hypnogogic state. Considering all the other wonderful things the human brain is capable of tricking itself into, getting yourself into a position where you will consistently believe and do what you're told obviously isn't all that difficult to do.

Your subject will, depending on your renown and a million other reasons, be somewhere between really and truly 'hypnotised' and really and truly not - and yet still act in perfectly the right way for you to carry out these deceptions.

'The Chi Sphere' - Hypnotic Induction Routine

Now that you understand the basics of suggestion we can start to look at ways of using it in your routines. But remember, a subject who feels that the routine you're doing is a challenge, and that he needs to pit his wits against your mentalist 'powers', isn't going to respond as you need him to. Instead, try to keep subtly promoting the idea throughout this routine that this is not a 'trick' but an experiment. The more your volunteer believes that the less he will try to see through the routine, and will instead want it to succeed - and feel like he's helping you perform too. Most subjects will actually want this trick to work anyway, as it's alluding to the existence of abilities within themselves that we all might hope for.

The paragraphs written in italics will tend to be explanations of the reasoning behind certain words in the scripting, or the overall psychology that is being promoted. Once you've understood this reasoning, read the text through again, but without the italic paragraphs so that you can get a better sense of the overall timing and flow of the routine.

Note for this first one that it'll be better if the subject doesn't wear any bulky rings or have sweaty hands.

Effect: You create an unseen sphere of 'Chi energy' between your hands and place it around your subject's outstretched arms, locking their hands together. No matter how hard the try they can't escape the power of the sphere you have created.

Opening script:

"The concept of Chi - a hidden, powerful energy within us all - is common to many ancient civilisations. In some people this energy is obvious, displayed through various feats of physical strength or mental powers. In others it's a subtle energy that manifests infrequently, usually at the hands of someone who can bring out this latent ability. As with all arcane, almost magical skills, there's only one real drawback for those who are lucky enough to possess higher than normal levels of Chi energy - that they in turn are more susceptible than others to the Chi of another person."

This is the provenance of the effect, saying that it isn't just a modern invention but an ancient skill/power. It alludes to a hidden power, Chi (or 'Ki' in Japan) that every subject hopes they may possess, making it a very attractive experiment not only to take part in, but to succeed within too. Chi is spoken of as being 'a power' and 'almost magical', instantly creating a compelling and mysterious atmosphere for the routine. It also establishes too the idea that the performer knows more about these esoteric ideas than the average person, inferring to some degree that he has unspoken abilities himself and has long experience in experimenting with them. You also say, 'it's a subtle energy that manifests infrequently, usually at the hands of someone who can bring out this latent ability', inferring that you are that person.

You turn to your volunteer and say, "If you're willing, what I'd like to do is just try to test the natural level of your Chi. It might feel a little strange, but it's not going to hurt. Would you mind taking part? If you feel scared or disturbed at any time just say and we'll stop, okay?"

This is inferring that it IS strange and that it may well be disturbing. Expectation.

To demonstrate you hold out both hands at about stomach height with the hand-blades pointing downward, palms facing each other. Slowly move your hands closer together, pausing as they get about a hands-width apart, then move your hands gently in and out as though you're trying to find something. At one point, you stop and feel at the air between your hands more carefully. You seem to find what you're looking for. You smile.

"Ah, there it is. Do you see that? It's different for everyone, but just about there...."

Now fix your subject eyes and say, "Don't worry, this should be quite easy. All you have to do is copy what I do and you'll feel it too. Just relax and see what happens..."

The act of looking them deeply in the eyes is significant to most people who have high expectations of hypnosis and magic, signifying to them that you are now beginning to exercise control. Make sure that you have rapport as you do this or looking into their eyes will be seen to signify that a challenge is about to begin, you against them. This will obviously have a detrimental effect.

Hold your hands apart as you did at the beginning of the routine and ask them to do the same, moving your hands slowly in and out as you talk.

"If you just move your hands together very slowly, when you get to about here (your hands are now about 12 inches - 30 cm - apart) you should feel a slight resistance. It'll be a bit like the push outwards you feel when you try to bring the same ends of two magnets together. In some people it's not very strong and a quite small sphere of energy. In others it can be as big as a basketball, which I've only seen a couple of times..."

Here you give the subject something to aim for; the idea that if they feel the sphere is as big as a basketball then that's an extremely good result for you and that you would be very pleased. It's also an indication, as you've stated, that this would be out of the ordinary, "I've only seen it a couple of times..."

Most will feel a repelling pressure at some point, and even those who don't will say that they have, if only briefly. This shows that they want to be seen to be successful in the routine and will happily continue to play along until they have something more tangible to believe in.

Remember, this is a test of susceptibility. The more strongly they seem to 'feel it', the better a subject they're going to make. They're showing that they're concentrating and listening to what you're asking them to do without trying to be obstructive. As for the reality of what they feel, it's a mixture of blood pressure and expectation that's used regularly in martial arts schools to show students how powerful their Chi is supposed to be.

Give them time to appreciate or find the supposed sphere, then say, "I'll show you something else pretty remarkable about this. Hold your arms out straight ahead of you like this-"

Hold both of your arms out parallel and at shoulder height and get them to copy you. When they've done so, link your hands together (as in Figure 4) and again get them to copy you. As you do this say, "As I said earlier, ancient cultures learned - for their own protection - that if someone tried to use their Chi powers for evil purposes the governing priests had ways of dealing with them that I'd like to demonstrate."

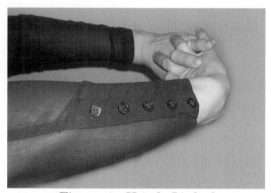

Figure 4 - Hands Linked

Demonstrate - not challenge. This helps further the idea that this is a co-operative experiment. You also make reference to the 'governing priests', that they had powers that you are now going to illustrate, inferring that you too have similar powers.

Make sure that their fingers are pushed tightly together. Run your hands up the outside of their arms (particularly on and above the elbow) without touching them, saying, "Nice and straight, solid. Keep them straight for me...That's good" Keep reassuring them that they're doing everything you need them too and that you're pleased with how things are going.

Now appear to locate the Chi Sphere between your own hands again. With a slow intake of breath appear to enlarge it to about the size of two basketballs. Another breath, let your eyes half-close and eyelids flutter, bring the sphere out again until its slightly bigger than the width the subject's arms are apart. Now, with great deliberation, hold the sphere in your hands and appear to slip it over the subject's arms until it rests at their elbows (see Figure 5).

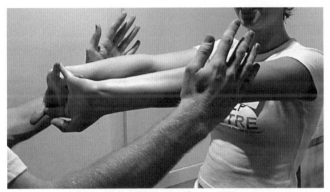

Figure 5 - Hands Over Elbows

Now you need to show the limits of the sphere. Move your hands around it, showing how it surrounds the subject's arms and elbows. Each time you pass your hands over their elbows keep affirming the suggestions that their arms are a straight line, stiff as an iron rod.

"The power of the sphere now encloses you arms and hands - for all intents and purposes locking your hands together until it's removed. Your hands are a single block of stone, held by the sphere.

Any distractions at this point can ruin the effect, so it's important that you keep the subject focussed. To best do this, point to one of your eyes and have the subject keep looking at it as you continue. Keep your hands close to their elbows as you say, "Now, keep your arms where they are. Straight, very straight. Now slowly, I want you to try and move your hands apart..."

The physical effect here is quite real. Nobody can move their hands apart whilst in this position, it requires the subject to lower their hands or move their elbows to do it. But you have your hands at their elbows, thus preventing them from doing this. As long as they're listening to your suggestions that they keep their arms straight there isn't a hope in the world that they can separate their hands. Be careful here that you don't say, "Pull your hands apart," or anything that would infer that they should try to snap them apart. If they do this in one movement, opening their elbows as they do so, there's a chance they might succeed.

Be aware too that some subjects will get very nervous about this sudden lack of control over themselves. Be supportive but authorative as they struggle to free their hands, making sure that they keep their arms straight and their fingers locked together.

"Just gently. You can feel it can't you? It's locking your hands together like they're a solid block of stone. Don't try to fight against it. The more you struggle the harder it'll be to get free from. Nothing bad will happen, I'm in complete control. Just relax and feel the power of this for a moment..."

Let them struggle a little longer then finish the effect by saying, "I'll now earth the Chi power and your hands will drop and immediately return to normal-"

Put your hands above their arms as you say this. Now clap your hands together just under their chin, saying, "Drop!". They'll drop their arms and, with some relief, get free from 'the sphere'. If they have trouble releasing themselves, which may well happen, gently part their elbows as you lower their hands, allowing them to move their fingers apart.

As an introduction to suggestion this is almost infallible and very easy to carry out. From here you could go into any standard routine to enforce the sense of 'power' you're conveying, or even simply do more similar, entertaining 'tests' that again use this idea of a sphere of energy, like the 'Chi Eye Lock', below.

Both the above and two following induction methods/susceptibility tests have been around for over a hundred years (though are usually explained without any theme or scripting of the kind we use here), but they're still excellent ways of getting the ball rolling with little risk of failure. It can be very entertaining if you're doing a casual routine for friends or at a small party to simply do all the tests we describe here, one after the other as a performance. Each is harmless, helps isolate key subjects and is very entertaining to watch - especially if you have multiple volunteers. If you do this we would end on something slightly different in style to end the act to avoid the feeling of same-ness.

The Chi Eye Lock

This is an alternative induction, again based on simple physical laws which are emphasised and directed by suggestion. This one can be very useful if you intend to go directly into a more hypnosis-led routine straight afterwards that requires the subject to have their eyes closed. The only real problem with this induction is that your subject needs to be sitting down throughout it.

Here the required eye position your subject will take up is used in some meditational forms to help create a calm mind - and can lead directly to altered states of consciousness if used correctly and with the right subject. Volunteers may of course not have the pleasure of entering into this kind of state but may still tend to become aware of feelings of floating, lacking physical boundaries, or of being 'locked in' to a state of deep pleasure, etc. Although the aim of the technique isn't to gain these experiences, any blurring of what the volunteer considers to be 'normal' perception can only help take the effectiveness of the routine to greater heights.

We again use the idea of 'Chi Energy' to drive this technique, if this isn't suitable to your approach simply rework the script accordingly. As long as the basics of suggestion are left intact it doesn't really matter what you attribute the effect to.

EFFECT: The seated subject is asked to close his or her eyes. The performer creates a sphere of energy and rests it against the subject's forehead, locking the subject's eyes closed until the performer removes it.

If this is the first induction you're doing in your performance, use the opening script from the previous routine to establish the credibility of what you're about to do. Having demonstrated how to create the sphere and allowed your subject to experiment with it too, move straight into the following;

Ask your subject to relax completely. Pay particular attention to their shoulders and head, placing your hand on or over each as you say, "Relax, fall. Let them go. Stay upright but let your whole body feel heavy, almost like it's going to sink right down through the chair." You'll need to reinforce the subject's sense of relaxation throughout this effect or it'll work less effectively.

As holding the required eye position steadily from cold is quite hard, you need to allow your subject an opportunity to get used to it first. Place your finger centrally, high on the subject's forehead. Ask the subject, with eyes open, to look upwards, as much towards the tip of your finger as they can, holding their eyes steady.
"Hold your eyes, still, but don't force them. All you need to concentrate on is looking upwards and relaxing, okay? Keep looking upwards and see how easily you can blink your eyelids when you need to..." As they blink, say, "That's good, your eyelids are free and normal aren't they? Stay relaxed, steady. Keep looking up..."

These phrases are establishing that looking upwards in no way impairs their ability to open or close their eyes, which will be important to them psychologically in the later phase.

Try to keep the person looking upwards for about a minute to get their eye muscles used to looking steadily upwards at this angle, then take your finger away. "Okay, relax and lower your eyes. You feel okay? Good. Now what I'm going to do is just create a (or 'another') sphere of Chi energy and I'm going to rest it on the bridge of your nose. I'm going to try to place the very centre of it on the Chakra at the middle of your forehead just to see what will happen. You'll find this is quite strange."

No promises of anything in particular happening here. Whatever occurs IS the effect as far as the subject is concerned; although we're going to concentrate mainly on locking their eyes shut.

Now you ask them to close their eyes. But, rather than have them close their eyelids and then look upwards, it's easier for them to look upwards and then close their eyes. They end up with half open eyes, the whites showing, but are still unable to see and far more comfortable with sustaining the upward position for any length of time.

Place your finger centrally between their eyebrows, saying, "Just look at the tip of my finger. Only the tip. Stay nice and relaxed. Let your shoulders drop like you did before. That's good. Stay looking at the tip of my finger..."

When their eyelids have stopped flickering, this is the signal that they're both comfortable and relaxed, allowing you to move on.

"I'm now going to create a sphere of Chi around the tip of my finger and place it against your forehead. You should be able to see right into the middle of it. Sometimes it contains a bright light, but it doesn't matter if you see this or not."

This gives them something to look 'into the sphere' for, keeping their attention inwards.

Let out a slow exhalation, thus giving an auditory signal that the sphere is now in place. "I want you to see the centre of the sphere resting just about - here...(press a little harder for a second)...Just relax and look up at it, keep looking up at the centre where you feel me touching. Keep looking forward into it. Nice and relaxed. Breathing gently. Now, slowly and gently, try to open your eyes. Keep looking at the sphere..."

The volunteer's eyelids will be fluttering as they try to open their eyes, but as long as they keep looking upwards it's physically impossible to do so. Of course that means that anyone who does open their eyes with ease isn't listening to your instructions, so in hypnosis you would move onto trying this on another subject. Keep giving steady, clear commands that they should keep looking at the sphere (and your fingertip) whilst trying to open their eyes - and if they're following you closely enough their eyes will be locked shut.

At this point, as with the earlier induction, watch for any panic in your subjects. You've just 'taken control' of their ability to function normally and some will definitely feel twinges of fear. Intersperse all commands with regular references to the subject relaxing and breathing steadily, which will help divert them and counter much of their anxiety.

"As you've discovered, the sphere holds your eyes shut. Tightly closed. Locked onto the single point at my finger. Your eyes looking upwards, your eyelids tightly closed..."

Hold the subject in this position until the spectators have had a chance to see how much they're struggling. To finish the induction - once you've clearly demonstrated to the subject (and audience) that he can't open his eyes, say;

"Now relax. Shoulders down, body relaxed, breathing slowly and gently. I'm going to remove my finger and the sphere of energy from your forehead and everything will be back to normal."

Breath out audibly again as a cue that the sphere has gone, then remove your finger from their forehead.

"Open your eyes!"

The subject will (though some with a little difficulty) now open their eyes.

Chi Card Attraction

Effect: The performer relaxes the subject before placing his hands against theirs, telling the subject that he is increasing their natural Chi energy to make it stronger and easier to detect at their feet and head. The subject is then given a playing card to hold between their fingertips, pointing it down towards the ground. After a little preamble, the subject begins to feel the card pulling in towards their own feet - and even tugging quite hard at their fingers - progressively growing heavier in their grasp. Once this has been demonstrated the card is pointed at the subject's head where it is felt to be drawn even more strongly upwards, it's pull appearing to lift the subject's arm into the air.

Begin by giving some background to this effect by saying that, as someone who constantly explores esoteric texts to find ways of increasing your abilities, you've discovered the following passage in a book on ancient magical arts. Rather than just say something like the following, it will add to the idea that it's a genuine text by having it written down on a piece of paper and reading from it.

"Let me just read you something: '...In the earliest years of the development of Shaolin Temple martial arts, it was thought that the greater a monk and warrior a student became the greater his inner vitality, his Chi, would become. One test used to establish a student's Chi level was relatively simple - strips of stiff rice paper about the length of a man's finger were held near the head or feet of the student; If the Chi was strong at either of these points the strips were said to be attracted towards the student's body, just as paper is attracted to silk-rubbed amber. This was of course an indication of the student's great latent powers...'"

Remember that this is the reasoning behind doing the whole routine, its validation as an effect. How you say this is important as it establishes certain elements within the subject's mind: the idea that there's a power within them that can and has been felt with pieces of card-like material since ancient times. The type of attraction they may feel happening - like 'silk-rubbed amber'; and the reference to Chi as being a 'great latent power', which we'll later infer that they may actually have.

Continue; "Now, in my experience, about 1 in 10 people already have a high enough level of Chi to be detected in this way, if you know how. Obviously I'm always intrigued to see if anyone I meet has that kind of ability. So, what I'd really like to do if you don't mind is to try an experiment to see how high your Chi level is right now. Would that be okay? It's just an experiment, nothing scary is going to happen to you, but I do realise that a lot of people will find it very odd to realise there's a hidden energy within themselves. It's a quite peculiar effect I have to say. There'll be no pressure on you though, and if at any point you feel that things are getting too much for you then we can stop straight away, alright?"

Establishing ideas in the Subject's mind: 1) This is a strange experiment that might scare some people. 2) It's a test of their 'hidden power'.

Ask any spectators to stay in complete silence for the following process, telling them that you need to be able to focus very intently on what you're doing.

Say to the subject, "Before we begin, it's very important that you relax and clear your mind. Stand up straight, head straight, look at me...that's good, relax more, drop your shoulders...just take a couple of long slow breaths... and now relax, particularly at your solar plexus and shoulders... good, that's fine. Try to stay relaxed...excellent..." Move your hands over the areas mentioned above as you speak, inferring that you have some kind of external control over what happens at them. As they begin to relax the volunteer will wonder, are you relaxing them or are they?

The places mentioned above are sources of tension in most people's bodies. Getting rid of these tensions in your subject will help him get into the mood of the effect and allow him to focus more clearly on what you're asking him to do. A relaxed body means a relaxed, receptive mind. (See also 'Relaxation').

Now, you have two choices: you could deliver the process above like a doctor, warmly but clinically and create good relaxation without any problem. On the other hand, if you deliver it as though it were an hypnotic induction in itself you're creating a volunteer who thinks they're on their way into some kind of hypnotic state before you've even begun to deliver any direct suggestion. Watch what the subject does to themselves as they're being relaxed. They're expecting something strange because what you're doing is unusual for a 'normal' trick. Nobody's mentioned hypnosis yet, but the inference will be that this is again the start of a 'something'. As you guide them deeper into relaxation they'll continue to look out for odd frames of mind or sensations, becoming much more open to suggestion as they do so. As long as you avoid defining exactly what sensations are meant to occur, anything they find that they weren't previously aware of in the normal workings of their mind may now be misinterpreted by them as something novel and an indication that they're moving deeper into a special state.

Also, even though the routine you're about to do doesn't involve suggestion at all, you infer by using a 'hypnotic' delivery that you need them in a different state to perform it - and thus take the trick onto a new level in their minds. It's no longer just a simple magical effect, but something much more. If you did a standard card trick with the same relaxation sequence at the beginning of it, what would it imply to the subject about the effect? Nobody's said a word about hypnosis. They have no idea what you're doing as you're relaxing them, but they'll draw their own conclusions about why you've taken this particular approach and decide that what you're doing must involve some deep psychological techniques. It's not a bad thing, it's just striking how the subject can fool place themselves into a suggestible state just by thinking that the relaxation process has special meaning.

Once you think your volunteer is relaxed, ask him to raise both hands to solar plexus height, palms facing you. After a few seconds of 'mental preparation', look your subject deep in his eyes and place your palms against his.

Say quietly, "Okay, what I'm going to do is add a little of my Chi to your own. Don't worry, it might feel a bit odd, but you'll be fine. What will happen is that this extra energy will tend to accumulate at your head and feet for a while, allowing you to feel it more strongly there, okay? You wont feel any bad effects and in fact most people say that they feel quite revitalised for a while afterwards..."

Still looking your subject in the eyes, let your own eyes defocus as you relax and give an audible exhalation through your half-open mouth.

Continue silently appearing to 'project your Chi into him' in this way for a few more seconds, then stop and lower your hands, looking quietly pleased with the result.

Although you might think that we're overplaying looking into the subject's eyes so frequently, it really does play an important role in these effects. Because of the little that most people know about hypnosis and the like they'll equate it with the assertion of power. But even with no knowledge of hypnosis we all subconsciously know that looking directly into someone's eyes is a non-verbal indication of power too. Like it or not, many will feel put under pressure, or even that they're being 'controlled' by you if you sustain it at the right times.

"That's good - very good in fact. I think you should do well....The next thing we need is a modern counterpart of the ancient 'strip of stiff rice paper' - an ordinary playing card."

Now hand the subject a playing card and ask them to hold it lightly near one end between their thumb and fingertip, the bulk of its length pointing downwards (see Figure 6). Position their hand about a third of a metre away from their solar plexus, making sure that neither the hand nor arm are supported by resting on their body. Turn their elbow away from their body so that the card is squarely facing the subject.

Figure 6 - Card Pointing Downwards

Getting the subject's eyes in the right position will help too, for reasons we'll explain in a moment. Try to make sure that their heads are relatively upright and that their hand is in such a position that they have to look downwards at about 45 degrees to watch it. Throughout this, direct them to make certain that they're standing squarely, and that they're still looking at the card at the desired angle.

Continue, "Keep looking steadily at the card. Relax, let your shoulders fall...Hold the card lightly. In a few seconds, as long as you're relaxed, you'll feel a definite pull on the end of the card, in towards your own feet. This will start off as just little tugs at your fingertips, growing progressively stronger over the space of a couple of minutes as you tune your mind to the Chi. Don't slacken your grip too much on the card once it begins or it'll slip through your fingers. You need to maintain the contact between your energy and it's. But don't hold too hard either, your grip will stop you sensing the movement of the card altogether."

You're giving clear instructions about how tightly to hold the card, which is important if this effect is to work. It's basis is very simple; any slight movement of their hands will cause the card they hold to vibrate slightly; and these vibrations in turn are amplified along the length of the card they hold. Even the simple pulse of blood in their hand and fingers will be felt as small downward tugs (or upward, depending upon what you're telling them they'll feel), so you want the participant to be highly focussed on being aware of holding the card and looking out for these movements.

Pace the above and all the following statements carefully. Obviously, don't just say what we've said here without a pause. Pace each phrase and give the subject time to take in what you're saying. Let it have an effect on them. Don't hurry.

Remember, in this kind of routine the subject may be highly attuned to what you say and the way you say it. Any subtle under-currents of double meaning, ridicule or hesitance will be all the more noticeable to them. If there's any hesitation in your voice it'll sound as though you're not quite sure of what you're doing. If there's a slight smile in your voice it might seem to them as though you're not taking what you're doing - or them -

very seriously. Aim to sound sincere and co-operative, avoiding too much dominance. You're both trying to make something work.

It may seem like a contradiction to say that the subject is more highly aware of what you say in this type of effect rather than in one that just uses Sleight of Mouth. But there's a real difference between using suggestion hidden in linguistic deception and giving the subject obvious direct orders as we do here.

As they're looking at their card, you watch it intently too and, after a pause, say, "I can see it starting to move inwards. You can feel it can't you? Keep looking at the card, I want you to see this too. Keep looking steadily at your fingers."

This is confirming the subject's belief that any tremors they at least think they saw or felt can be seen by someone else too. Even if they don't believe in what you're doing you'll have created a small element of doubt about whether they were paying attention in the moment you were talking about. Would you really say something like that if it wasn't true? You're a performer, yes, but would you really say something bold like, 'your finger moved' in front of a lot of other people who were also watching closely too? It makes the subject think, What did he see? What did I not see?

With a good subject they'll begin to feel movements starting after less than a minute. Watch their expression for any sign that they can actually feel the card pulling on their fingers, then say, "See - it's happening! Is it tugging? That's good, just try to stay nice and relaxed. Can you feel it pulling down? What's it doing?"

Pace statements like these, using your own words wherever possible to keep it sounding natural. A little at a time.

If it's already working and you need to deepen the effect, say, "This usually begins to affect the elbows of some people first, are you feeling anything there? Like a weight around your elbow? I've seen this making someone's arm so heavy they couldn't hold it up. I don't know if that will happen here..."

That someone was so affected by this that they couldn't hold their arm up is a piece of subtle psychology, and it should give them the subconscious understanding that ultimate outcome for you is for their arm to be too heavy to hold up. They'll realise that if it happens to them too, they instantly become amongst your 'best' subjects. This will be a very attractive idea to certain types. Suggestion, in a good subject, works because of their desire to please the performer.

They'll now begin to notice that holding their arms out like this is getting pretty tiring. Is it just because the arm is heavy and it's been there for a long time? Or is it because what you're telling them really is happening? Now they have doubts about their own objections, if they had any - and affirmation that this is something very strange if they didn't.

Follow this after another pause (in which you're still watching the card, enthralled) with, "You'll tend to feel your hand and arm getting heavier and heavier the more strongly the card begins to pull. Do your best to hold it up for a while to see how strong the Chi gets, I'm pretty intrigued to see how far it might go!"

Again, if you've chosen a good subject the supposed weight of the card will start to pull down very quickly. When it does happen, give the subject enough time to feel how powerful it might seem. "You can feel it tugging can't you? That's quite strong, isn't it?"

How strong is strong? What can they base a reasoned reply on with no previous experience of a weak or strong tug...?

Once the imaginary weight of the card has been felt by the subject to a good degree - and that you're sure that this fact has been appreciated by your audience, get ready to move to the next part of the routine. How well they respond to this effect will of course vary considerably, so don't always hold out for getting them to a point where they can't hold their arm up any longer. If they're grimacing against the weight of the card, or showing any other obvious signs of discomfort that's all you need to show the audience that the routine has working successfully, and you can then move on.

Hold one of your hands near to the card and say, "Okay, you're doing really well, but I don't want to tire you out or exhaust the Chi we've built up, so I'm going to just short-circuit the effect and drain away the Chi from the card by earthing it through my own body, okay? As soon as I do that the pull will disappear completely. Ready?"

Slowly and gently touch your finger to the card and draw in a small breath through your open mouth. "There, that's it. Can you feel the card returning to normal now? Good. Okay, just relax again...how did that feel?"

It really doesn't matter if they respond or not. Unless they really don't want this to work they only have two choices if they do reply. They can choose to acknowledge that they felt their hand 'returning to normal', in which case they've shown that it was previously 'abnormal' and affected by Chi; or risk saying they didn't feel anything at all, admitting that they don't have the power the Mentalist had hoped to find.

Given the chance to respond, most will agree that they at least felt 'something', but will be unable to say what exactly. Even this vagueness is excellent validation of the trick for your audience.

Now continue, "If you thought that was a bit strange I'd now like to show you an even more powerful effect along the same lines, this time with the Chi that's accumulated at your head. This is going well, so don't worry...But if you don't want to continue that's okay, you've demonstrated the effect I wanted us to show the audience already, so it doesn't matter if you're finding this odd...Are you okay to continue?"

The subject will, 9 times out of 10, want to go on. If not that's just as useful because the spectators will have watched you do something that the subject found so strange they don't want to continue.

If they choose to go on, ask them to hold the card again in the same way as before, but this time with the bulk of it pointing upwards. If necessary, position their hand and fingers for them, tilting it so that the card rests against the ball of their thumb tip (see Figure 7).

Figure 7 - Card Pointing Upwards

Continue, "Now this really is strange. You're going to feel the card almost lifting your hand upwards, then your arm will begin to get lighter as well..."

Allow the subject to get used to the change of direction and experiment with the card for a few moments, then encourage them again by saying, "You can feel it already, can't you? I can see your arm bouncing slightly as it's being drawn upwards. Can you feel your hand getting lighter too? Excellent...! It looks like it's getting lighter and lighter...! Isn't that strange?!? "

If the subject is slow in responding give them a little more time to get into the swing of what you're doing. Some people are more cynical than others, and even if they want to comply with you in this 'experiment', there'll still be an element of doubt about it in their minds until they decide whether what you're doing is 'real' or not.

As the effect deepens, avoid allowing them to experiment with letting the card 'fly up' from their fingers (as it will feel that it wants to do). Say, "I know as it gets lighter that the temptation is just to let the card float free of your fingers by itself, but I'd like you to maintain contact with it at all times otherwise the link between you and it will be broken and it'll just fall to the floor."

Don't forget that no matter how well they seem to be doing you still need to keep enforcing the suggestion that their hand and arm are getting lighter. Continue along the following lines in between giving more direct instructions on what to do with the card. Timing is important here. Stagger each of your suggestions about the card weight to allow them time to get used to each new idea.

"Your arm really is getting lighter isn't it? This is a much more profound effect in the right people...It's pulling inwards quite strongly now..."

If their arm is now visibly and steadily rising, give the subject another 'best case' goal to aim for. "Normally it wouldn't go this high. I've only seen it better than this once or twice...."

Try to sound sincerely pleased about the way things are going. If they feel that they're already meeting or even surpassing your expectations, many subjects will rise to the occasion (no pun intended!) and allow themselves to be carried away by the effect.

When you're ready, raise your hand near to theirs again and say, "I don't want to use too much of this up, because there's something else that we can do with it that will absolutely amaze you...I'm just going to drain the Chi away from the card again and I'll show you..."

Touch your finger or hand against the card as before and, solemnly, take in another breath of air, saying, "There it goes. Can you feel it going back to normal?" They will nod, say 'yes', or simply gape at this point. "Good, that's fine...Now you can relax and lower your hand..." Smile to the audience and say, "I think that deserves a round of applause, don't you?"

This might sound a normal bit of showmanship, to court applause from the audience. But really what you're saying here is that the subject has contributed to the effect and has done well, making all the more certain that they will try to co-operate just as well in the next effect you do.

Why this works...

We're working on two levels with this routine. A physical effect is perceived as enhanced through suggestion, which in turn increases the depth of that effect, misdirecting the subject as to its cause. Suggestion by itself would still do the trick, but having real physical sensations to support that suggestion is ideal.

If you hold a card as the subject would in the first part of the routine (pointing downwards), you'll notice a slightly heavier pressure on your thumb tip than your finger that makes it feel to like the card really is pulling in towards your feet. This is due to the fact that you will always hold the card slightly away from being straight up and down - and the thumb will always bear most of the pressure of that vertical imbalance. As the subject focuses his awareness on his fingertips he becomes aware of this pressure and, as he has his thumb on the side of the card nearest his body, the pressure will seem to be directed in that direction. Also because the card he holds is extended from his fingers, its length amplifies any other movements his hands make. Small pulses of blood and any tiny tremors his hands make will further press on the card, giving the impression of something pulling at it.

Don't keep this all going on too long, try to judge how entertaining the reaction of the subject is for your audience. If the subject isn't very demonstrative - though the effect is working - you might cut this first routine a little shorter once you feel you've established good impressionability. And that's important to remember; not only are you trying to do a routine, you're also involved in an ongoing process of deepening your subject's impressionability.

It isn't possible to give a hard and fast time for how long it takes for any subject to feel these movements; and then decide that they're something other than what they are. It depends on a number of factors, such as:

• Their ability to focus their mind on their thumb and fingers, away from what's happening to them (being on stage, feeling nervous, wondering if they can do things they're asked to correctly, etc.)
• Their level of compliance. Are they feeling challenged by you in any way?
• How do they see you? Despite them being a volunteer, and even though they might be very ready to carry out any *physical* request you make, them believing what you say about why it's all happening may rest on your personality and image alone. Though we don't personally think it's necessary, it has helped many people's careers to be thought of as mysterious, or to describe the things that they do as being esoteric in some way. Mystery creates a sense of dominance, a presence of 'other' in you that people can feel slightly awed by. It's certainly useful to look for subjects who, for whatever reason, already may feel subordinate to you. This idea of dominance and challenge is the reason why most of you wont be able to hypnotise (should you have such relatives at hand to practise upon, poor souls...) your elder brothers, sisters, parents or wives and husbands. For you to suddenly say to them one day, "I've learned to hypnotise people and want to do it to you," would never work. They would never believe that you could get such a 'power' after them knowing you so long. But maybe the thing they'll object to most is the idea that you really *might* be able gain control over them, thus challenging their own perceived dominance over you, if it exists. If they feel superior to you in any way they're going to do everything to make certain that being hypnotised by you is NOT a possibility. This is obviously not an ideal situation to develop suggestibility in...☺

Eye Positions

The reasoning behind the eye positions we describe above is quite interesting. In practising some types of meditation the practitioner will be asked to adopt a particular level of gaze, usually with half-closed eyes. One of these levels is (with head upright, but chin slightly drawn in) to look downwards at an angle of about 45 degrees towards a point on the ground around 3 feet away. Now, funny things happen when you do this, especially if you're in the right frame of mind. You grow very focussed, but internalised away from outside distractions - a perfect state for your subject to be in as you talk to him or her. If you put the thing you want them to look at so that it's in this same line of sight it'll help them stay with the object/hand in a much clearer and steadier way. More focussed, but still quite able to listen to and act upon your commands.

It helps in other ways too. The movement of your eyes is directly linked to the flow of your thoughts, as your mind produces a new set of thoughts for every new thing it sees. Obviously then, holding a steady gaze conversely helps slow thoughts. If the subject has a steady mind they're more likely to be relaxed and listening fully to what you're asking them to do. Holding your eyes steady is also much easier to do when they're in this downward angle, implying some early purpose for it and the resultant frame of mind in our very early ancestors, perhaps to make it easier to forage at ground level. Although you might think it's going a bit far to use subtle devices like this, you want a subject with as calm and happy mind as possible, so anything you can do to instigate that has got to make your routines more successful.

12

Getting the Basics Right

Tone of Voice

During hypnosis the subject's eyes are closed and all their attention becomes concentrated on their other senses, particularly hearing. Every aspect of the performer's voice is then noted much more closely by the subject and given far more meaning. In mentalism your subjects, even without their eyes closed, are also going to be very aware of what you're saying to them and how you're acting, simply because they're the centre of attention and in a strange situation. What you say and when is therefore critical. One bit of misinterpreted off-the-cuff humour on your part, one wrong wording or apparent misplaced emotion and it's over.

If you're trying to give suggestions verbally (particularly if, for whatever reason, the subject's eyes are closed) you've got to try to iron out the remotest 'smile' in your voice. Think about it. You're on a chair, eyes closed, surrounded by people and somebody's trying to hypnotise you. It's all going well until you notice that, just for a split second, there was a trace of a smile in the performer's voice and maybe even a stifled giggle from someone in the audience. What would you do? You'd instantly wonder what had happened - and probably think too that what everybody was finding funny was you. End of performance. Be very aware of every nuance and potential inference of what you say to your subjects.

Pacing

When you're experimenting with suggestion, plan your script, keep it natural. Not too wordy, no challenges. In hypnosis, pacing gives regular information for the subject to base what they do and perceive upon. Continual and easy to understand instructions that they can listen to without any effort. Effort is aroused and the effect spoiled if the subject notes any hesitation, or worrying emotion, etc., in your voice. It draws them away from their relaxed and open (to suggestion) state. If you try any of the later techniques you'll see how important it is to keep talking, giving commands as the subject needs them, but pay close attention to pacing. They'll feel awkward during overly prolonged silences, or confused if you're asking them to think about or do too much at once. Watch out too for noisy spectators, one cough or half-heard whisper is easily enough to put a subject off unless you can quickly give them another instruction to think about to take their minds of the interruption. Pace any suggestions to the subject's needs.

Also, put some work into getting your tone and inflection right. No need for weird monotones, just calm, clear-paced commands and instructions. As long as what you say has the right content and is *at that moment* within the bounds of what the subject can accept as being true then they will believe it. Nobody can be made to do something they would not normally do, but they can be made to believe that their world has sudenly gained some extraordinary new possibilities if you use suggestion correctly.

Let's now just review a synopsis of the other basics of suggestion that we've already covered:

- Where possible, use induction methods to discover the most susceptible amongst your volunteers.

- Remove the idea that anything you're doing could be construed as a challenge to your subjects. This is not a war of wills, but a co-operative experiment.

- Build self-doubt and uncertainty in your subject's mind about the validity of his or her normal perceptions with one or more induction techniques or any appropriate mentalist trick before moving onto those effects that use suggestion alone (such as the later 'arm-raising' effect). If they've been fooled once, they'll be much easier to fool a second time. Note that we aren't suggesting by this that you aim to destroy your subject's self-esteem irrevocably. It goes without saying that 'self-doubt and uncertainty' in this case mean purely within the confines of the effect and are used to increase the depth of the subject's suggestible state, not to destroy his confidence permanently!

• Create expectation.

• Confidence of delivery, plus good intonation and pacing of vocal content. Are you speaking gently and steadily? Not too theatrical, no long breaks, or overly repeated phrases? Above all, look out for ambiguity in what you say that the subject or audience might find funny. Laughter in the wrong place can be a real killer. Keep them relaxed but serious.

• Good scripting - rehearse!

• Fool as many senses as possible at once to make the illusion more effective. Layer suggestion.

• Rapport. Do your subjects like you?

• Create rapport, but also when necessary, try to aim for a level of subtle authority over your subject that they won't find intimidating.

• Relaxation - Make sure your subjects are as relaxed as possible. Physical tension leads to a lack of focus on your instructions and poor response times. Have you allowed your subjects enough space to get over any 'stage fright'? As the centre of attention they're going to be confused, embarrassed and a little self-conscious. Give them clear commands on how to relax as soon as possible to take their minds off worrying about whether they look stupid or not. As soon as they are relaxed, don't give them too much to do or think about - this will take them straight out of the relaxed state. To keep relaxation going, always move gently into the induction phase, avoiding disturbing them too much. Eventually you'll be able to spot subtle signs of physical tension appearing in your subjects (shoulders rising, fists clenching, increase in respiration rate) and will learn to intersperse relaxation commands with suggestions in your induction routines without them sounding out of place.

- Timing - are you allowing your subjects time to understand and then respond to your commands?

- Suggestion - Are your suggestions clear and unambiguous? Your subject must understand at all times what's expected of him. This must sound like we're stating the obvious, but it's easy for a someone in front of an audience to get confused if you don't give him or her time to understand what you say to them. You need to present instructions to them in logical little bites that they can easily perform without too much thought and effort when nervous or embarrassed.

- Don't try to be too subtle with your suggestions. Trying to feed a subject an image of going to sleep or the name of a playing card with commands and suggestions hidden carefully in your perfectly stressed lines will work with only a handful of people. The average subject simply may not hear, let alone subconsciously act upon, suggestion that is too subtle. This is NOT to say that *linguistic deception*, 'sleight of mouth' (rather than hypnotic suggestion) can not be delivered in a much more indirect way and with far less subtlety. People rarely notice how much they manipulate and are in turn themselves manipulated by words alone.

- Layering - Rule number one of hypnosis is that nobody can be made to do anything they don't want to, but we'd also add to that that they won't believe anything they don't want to either. All the suggestions you make must be feasible at that moment to the subject. However, if you've layered suggestion correctly - and more so after you've also done a powerful effect on them - you can extend what the subject believes and WANTS to believe is feasible. Don't be over-ambitious with your first effect or induction with any volunteer. Give them time to get used to everything that's happening to them, from being the centre of attention to learning how to be 'hypnotised'.

Although the following three principles of the use of suggestion apply primarily to hypnotic procedures, they're still the key to gaining successful subject responses in mentalism too.

Law of Concentrated Attention - whenever attention is concentrated repeatedly on an idea/suggestion, the idea tends to spontaneously realise itself.

Law of Reversed Effect - the harder you try to will yourself to do something you believe that you can't do, the less chance you have of succeeding.

Law of Dominant Effect - Attaching a strong emotion to a suggestion tends to make that suggestion more effective.

13

Pure Suggestion

The Law of Reversed Effect

Emile Coue, the father of auto-suggestion said, *"Whenever there is a conflict between the will and the imagination, not only do we not do that which we wish, but we do the exact opposite." Put simply, if you think that you would like to do something but feel you can't, the more you try the more difficult the task becomes."*

A common example of this is evident in people with insomnia. They expect not to be able to sleep and therefore don't - a prime example of how we can easily prevent ourselves from carrying out even the simplest of actions because of our belief that we can't do them.

Whereas the previous methods employed suggestion backed up by real physical sensations to create their effects, we're now going to look at techniques that use suggestion alone. Although this makes them harder to accomplish successfully on a regular basis, having to work at using your skills of persuasion make them far more gratifying to perform. How well the following routine is, as before, very dependant for its success on things like your level of rapport with the subject, performance setting, length of time available to create any previous Inductions, etc. If you have all the preliminaries in place then it will work 4 times out of 5, at least to some degree. Choose your subjects well and you can guarantee a 5 out of 5.

Does the potential for the failure of routines like this make them unusable in your performance? No, we really believe that it doesn't, especially if you can prime your audience to *expect* that they might not work. If they were to fail in a 'street magic' setting that might be seen as a real blow to your performance. But in a larger party or club situation where you can fit each effect into a longer routine, your failure is less critical. As we pointed out earlier, failure can in fact enforce the idea that you are using methods that have no certain outcome, and therefore (in the eyes of the audience at least) you can't be using methods that don't use props or trickery that would ensure they worked every time. The effect not working can then be put down to a wrong subject, lack of attention, whatever. An easy way to ensure a much higher success rate is to simply perform each routine on two subjects at once. Very few performers will be so unlucky as to choose two unresponsive volunteers.

However, be aware that suggestion works both ways. If subject 'A' sees that you're having no success with subject 'B' then that may negate some or all of the potential effects your suggestion has on subject 'A'. The way around this is to distance 'A' from the negative influence of seeing that what you're doing isn't working on 'B'. Take pains at the beginning of the routine to reinforce the idea that any effect that works well is a success for them as subjects too. If you impress upon them that for any of this to work they have to be imaginative, well focussed and intelligent, that implies that if it doesn't work on them then they're not any of these things.

Of course you don't want to make 'B' feel bad if what you're doing isn't working on him, but 'A' (and the spectators) need to know that this failure isn't due to hypnosis not being 'real', or that you lack skill in any way. But in fact, having 'B' fail can make the effect work even more strongly in 'A', as he tries to show that he's complying in exactly the way you want him to and is therefore a better subject. Remember, much of this is about the subconscious desire of the subject to work to the need and expectations of both performer and audience. In the right setting and with the right subject these routines work simply because the subject doesn't want to be seen to fail, or would feel uncomfortable making *you* fail by not acting exactly as you say they will. Imagine getting a volunteer on stage in front of a theatre full of people who have paid good money to see you and who love your work. Regardless of whether the subject is hypnotised or not they will do their best to make you look good. The more well-known you are and the more your reputation has preceded you, the less likely anything you do is to fail because of uncooperative subjects. They've paid to come and see you, so the last thing they want to do is to spoil your show and incur the wrath of someone they admire.

Down at a more normal level, where you may not have the pleasure of being a known performer, you have no such guarantees. But, beyond all of the who does what and why, once you find that real gem of a subject, he or she *will* be completely 'under your power' if you play them well. And you could wish for no more. You can have them unable to move or speak or forget their own names and where they live. These people, who respond quickly to every suggestion you make, may appear only once in a while, but when you do get one be ready to make use of them.

Some performers happily use the 'Paying Stooge' method to get them through a 'hypnosis' act. It's easily achieved and has resounding success. All you have to do is say to the subjects in a quiet aside that if , "You play along with me we can have a lot of fun with the audience..." The subject may (or may not) then dance and sing and do just about anything you want - and of course it makes for a good performance. But if you're billing yourself as a Mentalist with 'real powers' then every time you perform you're telling a small but important part of your audience that at least some of what you do is just play acting. We don't know about you but personally we don't feel safe with that approach and would rather just take our chances doing this stuff and seeing how it comes out, failures and all.

Floating arm effect

This is a very simple suggestion routine that, although it can take a little more time than the previous techniques to induce, produces a very visual effect and usually no little wonder in the mind of the subject.

Seat the volunteer on a chair beside a small table that allows them to rest their arm upon it (see Figure 8) comfortably without support. Make sure it's neither too high nor too low, the elbow should really *just* be in contact with the surface of the table. It's easier to do this one if the subject has their arm bare, but if that's not possible it will still work. Have them relax completely and put their palm on the table top, fingers extended but relaxed.

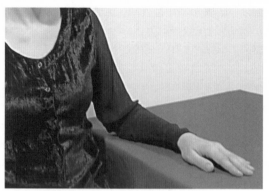

Figure 8 - Seated at a Table

Say, "What many people don't realise is that the idea of 'animal magnetism' is a real one. That living flesh and bones can be made to act like a magnet, either drawing things closer or pushing them away if it's used correctly. I'd like to demonstrate just how powerful that kind of attraction can be. I'd like you to imagine yourself as being a kind of human magnet. Although this isn't quite correct in an esoteric sense, we can roughly say that your 'North Pole' - your positive, attracting force is at your head. Your negative, repelling force is at your feet. If I attune myself to either of these poles we can get some quite remarkable things to happen. I have to say at the outset that in many people who are able to concentrate well this effect can be quite rapid, so I don't want you to be scared about the way this is going to feel. You're still okay with this? Good!"

Expectation and goal setting. 'Remarkable things will happen', and 'the effect can be quite rapid (if you're a good subject).

"Let's try for some positive effects firstly. What I need to do for a second if you don't mind is just absorb the energy excesses around your head. For want of a better word I'm going to 'magnetise' my hand and turn it into an 'attractor' to draw your flesh towards me. Anyone can try this kind of thing, you just need a little practise and a quiet atmosphere."

'It always works - if you know how'. If the subject gets home and tries it and it doesn't work, the reason is, as far as they are concerned, that they simply don't know how to do it correctly.

Place one open palm about six inches to the side of the subject's head. Make sure you get and maintain eye contact, preferably fixing your gaze on the bridge of the volunteer's nose. This gives your eyes a quite unusual quality that will help with the illusion. Take a couple of slow, audible breaths as you 'absorb their energy'. Now nod to yourself as though you're happy with the result and lower your hand.

"Okay, that's good - quite (look at your hand and raise your eyebrows as though you're surprised by what you've found)...powerful in fact."

Short as it is, this is a very loaded statement. Through this you've told the subject not only that they're 'above normal', but you're also inferring that you're now confident that what you're doing is going to work. This will help them remove any self-doubt about their ability to perform correctly and boost their confidence.

Take a moment to 'prepare yourself'. Don't go overboard with theatrical gestures, this should be subtle but show that this is something you've practised and consider to be real. Withdraw into yourself for a few moments. A deep breath. Really believe that your hand is now filled with 'attractive energy'. Hold it out in front of you almost like it's a burning stick of dynamite and keep it there as you continue.

"I want you to stay relaxed, don't rest on your elbow but don't try to support it either. Relaxed and aware. All you have to do is listen carefully and be aware of the way the skin on your arm feels for now. I don't want you to help me in any way, this really wont need you to do anything other than listen to my voice as you stay relaxed and aware. I don't even have to touch your arm, you could well feel my hand above yours from quite a distance away. Just watch for any kind of strange sensations as I'm doing this."

Now move your hand *slowly* towards the volunteer's outstretched arm as it rests on the table. Make use of anticipation at this point. You've built up the introduction to the effect and may well cause a psychosomatic effect of some kind in your subject as soon as your hand nears them. As your hand reaches a position over theirs, (staying at a height of about a couple of inches/4cm or so above it), and wait.

"As I move my hand over the length of your arm you'll begin to feel it moving over the surface of your skin even though I'm not touching you at all." Begin to slowly sweep your hand up towards their elbow. Take your time, saying as you do this, "You're already very sensitive, aren't you?"

No need for a response, this simply demonstrates that you can feel a connection between you both, even if the subject can't. If they do reply it will rarely be in the negative, and will seem to the audience as though they're saying they can already feel your hand moving above their arm. Now move your hand down toward their wrist, making slight movements as you do so as though you were really connected to the arm and lifting it into the air.

"You don't have to do anything now except watch what's happening. You'll feel your arm moving, becoming lighter as I move my hand over it, drawing it upwards..."

You should take pains to make it look as though you're working with a real force emanating from the subject's arm. Appear to grasp at an unseen energy from time to time, taking in a handful of empty air and pulling it upwards a few inches. The more you seem to believe this is happening the more they will too. Your hand movements are of course visual suggestions and therefore extremely important to keep going.

"Sometimes the lifting movement will start from the elbow, sometimes from the fingers...It's getting lighter and lighter, all the way along the length of your arm."

As always the response time will vary from subject to subject, but you may get results within a minute or so. If the subject is being slow, focus mainly on the hand and add some other suggestions to get the process rolling. Look out for any small twitches of their fingers and make the most of them.

"Look, it's starting to happen. Did you see that? It's getting lighter now."

When the first real signs of movement happen you're off and running. Remember to keep an eye out for which end of the arm it's beginning at and enforce this movement by further suggestion.

"Once this starts it will really feel as though your arm isn't your own. It gets lighter and lighter and will just rise into the air by itself as it's drawn towards my hand."

Look out for the arm raising too unevenly; if the arm 'sticks' to the table at the elbow or hand, use more suggestions to raise that too. Although it's a very dangerous route to take - and one that most hypnotists will warn against - it can in some cases help to get the effect going if the subject is being a little slow by saying that you can see movements before they have really started happening. Again the subject may believe that something has taken place that they might not have noticed. That one, unseen effect is sometimes all it takes to prove to the subject that this will really work.

"See? It's starting now. Don't help it, you don't need to. This will just rise up getting drawn towards my hand, lighter and lighter..."

Keep moving your hand slowly back and forth over their forearm as you speak. When the volunteer's arm eventually reaches a comfortable height about level with their shoulder, take your hand away.

"Your hand and arm are light, almost as though they belonged to someone else. It'll now stay there until I earth it and return it to normal.

Did you raise it up yourself? Are you holding it in place now?"

Answers to both questions will always be a very surprised, nervous, "No!"
"Can you lower it?"
"No!"

So the arm's in the air. What next? Well, as this can either be an induction or an effect in its own right you can either stop and take the applause or move into something else. But after all the set up why not continue to use the idea of attraction and repulsion further, by sticking one hand to the table whilst the other is in the air? Or how about having them stand and have you push them over or attract them with nothing more than a little suggestion and an upturned palm to act as a 'flesh magnet'? Anything that you want to do with your subjects will now be much easier to pull off now that they've felt your unaccountable 'power' first hand. By the time you get to a stage where you can do the above effect easily, you have an endless choice of further routines to draw on for further material. Most of these have formed the core of stage hypnosis acts for over a century, but as public displays of hypnosis have been all but banned in most countries for a long time now, it's doubtful that they'll have been seen (or *will* be seen) by any modern audience. This of course leaves the door wide open to anyone - like Derren Brown and others - who can adapt them to a mentalist setting and give them a new spin. Think how you might be able to use and update the following:

- Stop the subject speaking
- Have them fall forward/backwards
- Anaesthetise any area of skin
- Have an arm/leg too heavy to move
- Stuck to chair
- Eyes 'glued' shut
- Forgetting personal information

All of these techniques rely on exactly the same methods as those we've already talked about. All you need to do to implement any of them (once all the basics are out of the way) is to tell the subject what you're about to do, define a goal of best result to them, then continue with suggestion until the effect has been achieved.

Indirect Suggestion

Rather than working directly on the subject's mind/body in every routine, you can vary the presentation by seeming to use the 'mental powers' of the audience instead to give suggestion. Although the following is in essence just a simple variation on the above trick, we've built it up considerably with a simple introduction script and a relaxation sequence that everybody can join in on, giving the audience a sense of direct participation in the effect instead of just being observers. A routine is as big as you make it.

With a volunteer at hand, tell the audience;

"Many of the world's religions promote the idea that, rather than us all being individuals with our own minds and thoughts, we share a common consciousness, with our ideas of singularity just an illusion that we have created for ourselves. Some people call this common consciousness the Universal Mind and think of it as the very basis of our reality. A Oneness that we wrongly believe to be many.

"Now, if the Universal Mind really exists and we're all a part of a single consciousness, then isn't it possible that under the right conditions we could share thoughts and emotions? Isn't it also possible that, with guidance and force of numbers, we could perhaps influence the thoughts and even the body of another person? I'm sure you'd agree that it would be very interesting to find out.

"What I'd like to try to do is to see whether it would be possible for you to do this under these circumstances, to see if you can, as a group of people sharing one common goal, directly influence the thoughts and movements of another. The only involvement I'm going to have is simply to help you get in the right frame of mind and guide you through the process, the rest is up to you."

Remember to pace this script (or whichever one you decide to use - this is only an example of the way you *might* present this) and not just say it all as one long sentence. Take your time, give the audience enough time to co-operate and understand what you're trying to do. If they're still fidgeting after the following repeat some of the ideas once more to allow them time to settle down.

"Everybody relax, get comfortable, put your hands in your laps. Let your shoulders fall. Breath slowly, breathing in your lower stomach rather than in your chest. Deeper. Falling, relaxing, sinking down and down. Listen to your breathing, slow and gentle. Imagine breathing as one, thinking as one. All minds are one mind. One set of thoughts, infinite and open. Slower, more relaxed...good...Please, if you could all now try to hold onto that state, that idea of deep, heavy relaxation and try to stay completely quiet for the next few minutes. "

When everyone's quiet, turn quickly to your subject and have him stand facing the audience with his elbows raised to shoulder level, his forefingers extended with the tips pointing at each other but a little way apart. Now ask him to close his eyes. Make sure that the subject doesn't have his hands too close to his face or he may be able to see the shadows they cast on his closed eyelids - or feel his breath on his fingers - which would give clues about their position. Say firmly, "Our minds are joined as one, open yourself to the possibilities of shared consciousness. Don't resist any sensations you get. There's no need to worry about anything that happens, you'll be fine. Don't try to help us. Just allow yourself to be carried along by the minds here, okay?"

Don't try to help me, but 'Don't resist' and, 'allow yourself to be carried along'.

Turn again to the audience. "I need everyone to think about being relaxed, warm and happy. Breathing slowly. A single mind, one single intent. Everybody focus now on 'X's (your subject's name) left hand."

It will help if you indicate exactly which hand you mean here to avoid the confusion of, 'Does he mean my left or his?' It should always be the subject's left hand, and you might gently touch his left elbow just to let him know too that this is the one you mean.

"Imagine it lifting upwards. Think of clouds, feathers, a leaf on a breeze - anything at all that gives you an idea of floating and weightlessness. Imagine that you're making X's hand grow lighter and lighter, lifting it slowly into the air. Lifting, gently upwards. Floating, empty. Really feel as though it were your arm you were raising. Light, effortless..."

The subject's hand should start rising as you talk, but if it doesn't just keep reinforcing the idea of lightness in his hand for a few more seconds. Of course, although you're giving these instructions to the audience about what to try to project towards the volunteer, in fact your suggestions are still being directly obeyed by the subject, who would carry them out if the audience was there or not.

If the volunteer's hand hasn't moved, you have nothing to lose by saying, "Good. That's fine. See? It's starting. We can do this as long as we think as a single mind. Lifting, higher and higher."

Saying, "Good, that's fine. See?", makes the subject (who's eyes are thankfully closed) think that the effect is already taking place, thus helping to allay any doubts that he has over its effectiveness. He might have been waiting for a special sensation to signal the effect working, but if he feels it's already happening without any particular sensation occurring he can stop waiting and just get on with allowing his arm to do what he thinks it wants to.

Once his arm has been raised to your satisfaction you can then do the opposite on his other arm and try to make it so heavy that it becomes almost impossible to support. Once you have one arm up and one down, have the volunteer open his eyes to see the result. Most will usually be pretty astonished at what's taken place.

14

Wow! Surely I was Hypnotised?!

Martin: "I want to give you a very easy routine to do that, if done correctly, is extremely hard-hitting and baffling for any audience. On the surface it'll appear to be all about hypnotism, but in reality this is just clever trickery.

"Why use this routine you may ask when we've spent so much time explaining the how's and why's of doing the real thing? Because it's an easy way to establish your credentials as a 'hypnotist' or whatever you're trying to be, thus helping make sure that your later effects have a greater chance of success. It's all about getting people to be where you need them to be - and quickly. Why do six routines if you can do one routine instead to get them in the exactly same frame of mind? I know you might argue that we're cheating here. We are! But we're mentalists, that's what we do...

"So a few years ago I was in an upmarket restaurant with some existing and potential clients on a night out. Please note that I don't mention the fact that the restaurant was upmarket just for the sake of showing how stylish I can be, it just made the upshot of the story all the more painful, as you'll see. After having had a bit to eat and drink I got into doing magic, despite my better judgement and the sound knowledge that alcohol and magic rarely mix well. I quickly sensed that this audience wanted spooky and bizarre things to happen at the table rather than seeing the proverbial white rabbit pulled out of a hat - which was more than fine with me. Weird they wanted, weird they got. I did my stuff and it was going well, I couldn't seem to do any wrong.

"Maybe it was alcohol induced bravado, but I got to a point where I wanted to do a real kicker to astound them with; and I particularly enjoy routines where I stop my pulse. It's always a powerful experience for spectators and seems so impossible to do it scares most people half to death when they feel it happening, so I decided it was time to give my 'audience' a real thrill.

"Now, as you may or may not know, a common way to stop the pulse in your wrist is to place a small, hard ball in your armpit and squeeze this against your body so that it stops the flow of blood to your arm. But I've always found it rather annoying to have to walk around with a ball in my shirt ready to do this. I know some claim that it's possible to use your arm and chest muscles to surreptitiously squeeze the large vein in the armpit without the aid of a ball or anything else. Without commenting too much on this theory I will only say that I don't think this technique is possible for the great majority of us - so I do something else. I go to the toilet.

"The great thing about toilets is they are everywhere, and where there are toilets there is toilet paper. Toilet paper makes great balls of just the right density to use in this effect and they don't give me the same bruising in my armpit that I sometimes get from a plastic ball.

So, I went to the toilet and made a ball out of toilet paper, placed it in my armpit, then went back in to restaurant dining room ready to carry on. I'm pleased to say that despite the circumstances I did an excellent 'stopped pulse' routine. Everybody loved it. Nobody had a clue and I left everybody with open mouths. Applause to me. Perfect night...Or so I thought.

"When it was time to leave we paid up and were at the door of the restaurant. Just as we were getting outside one of my existing (luckily) clients came up to me and said, "Do you know you've got...erm...toilet paper hanging out your trousers?".

"I blanched and turned around - and sure enough I had a 3 metre streamer of paper hanging out my trousers that led back into the restaurant. I wish I could say that nobody noticed...

"As I tried to gather up the trailing paper snake someone asked, "What have you done?" I was just about to answer, "Remember that stopping pulse thing I did?" but I stalled. Despite me standing there with toilet paper hanging out my trousers people seemed impressed by what I had been doing at the table. I wouldn't, *couldn't* ruin that. So I went for the answer they were expecting. They still laugh and tell this tale to everybody who'll listen when we meet.

"Now for obvious reasons, after this I sat down to ponder whether I could do the pulse trick without any help at all. As I said above, I can't stop my wrist pulse by just squeezing my arm hard against my armpit so I had to think of something else. Before I continue I'd like to say that I still do the 'toilet ball trick' on a regular basis. It's an excellent effect and it's always there to use with the minimum of set up. Just be careful when you dump your ball of toilet paper...

Anyway, for this routine you don't need any props other than a pendant of some kind - the more esoteric looking this is the better. I use my own necklace, which is a rather strange looking one. It's an emblem symbolising my astrology sign in Celtic and on top of this I have an Egyptian 'Ankh' (Key of Life) pendant. I know it sounds like a complete confusion of style - and probably is - but I like it and can spin intriguing tales about this necklace if I need to. Anyway, find a participant. For this one you don't need to worry too much about rapport, just get a person who seems willing and co-operative. Sit them down, then sit down beside her. (I say 'her' in this case as this kind of thing gets the biggest response out of women for some reason.)

"Explain, "I'm going to try something with you. This is a bit strange and, as I don't want to put you in harm's way, I'll be the test dummy for this one. I should be okay, but I need you to focus as I can't do this for too long, okay? This is important!"

"Now you've established that something dangerous is about to happen, so dangerous in fact that you don't dare to use a volunteer for it. You've also established you've done this before and, as you're very keen on your own safety, you want to impress on her (and now she subconsciously knows) that it works, so she's prepared for any eventuality.

"Sit down beside her and show her your necklace, telling a tale about its history or its symbolism. Now explain, "In a minute I want you to find the pulse in my neck. When you've got it I want you to use your other hand to count out and illustrate the rhythm of my pulse, okay? When you've got a steady pulse I'm going to place my necklace in front of your eyes and swing it back and forth in time with it. Are you okay with this? Do you understand what I want you to do?"

"Ensure the instructions are understood and continue by saying, "I want you to keep your eyes on my necklace at all times, as I need you to monitor my pulse continuously - despite what might happen. Keep your eyes on the necklace and keep showing everyone my pulse rhythm with your other hand."

"You're emphasising here that things WILL happen, possibly even dangerous things. It's only a question of when.

"Continue, "When we begin I want you to tell me what you experience, what you feel. Anything you feel is worth mentioning you should state aloud. Are you okay with this?" Again ensure the instructions are understood. "Okay - let's proceed. Please find my pulse and show its rhythm with your other hand. While you're doing that I'll raise my necklace in front of you. From then on keep telling me what you experience".

"Place the subject's fingers on your mock 'pulse' (more on this in a second) to save time and to make sure that she's not listening to your real pulse. When she's got it and is accurately showing you and any audience present the rhythm with her other hand, bring out your necklace and swing it in a steadily, letting her watch its movements.

"Now here's the tricky part. Make your pulse move to the rhythm of your necklace for a few seconds then reduce its rate of swing a little at a time. As the necklace slows down in speed slow down your pulse accordingly. When the necklace has almost stopped moving, place it in your participant's lap - and stop your pulse. Take your time. Look detached from the world (she will look at you now even though you told her to only look at the necklace). Scare her. Wait. Now take up the necklace from her lap, set it in motion again and take a deep breath. Looking confused you start up your pulse in unison with the rhythm of the necklace.

"Cool trick, huh?

"Okay, obviously there is a bit more to it than I'm saying...! How to get the 'mock pulse' in the first place? Few people are aware that you can emulate your neck pulse incredibly well by placing your tongue flat against the roof of your mouth and pressing it rhythmically upwards. The movement will be so strong that your real pulse will 'disappear'.

"Now a few pointers. Play with this in front of a mirror and make sure that you aren't pressing too hard and making it obvious what's going on. Less is more. Place your own fingers on your neck and try it out. You'll be surprised how little movement of your tongue is needed.

"As I said, the 'tongue pulse' is stronger than your regular pulse and your regular pulse will simply disappear for the person feeling this. The way I use this routine I can actually get away with overdoing it as I place myself beside the participant. They won't watch me but the necklace. It's actually very easy getting your "tongue pulse" into sync' with the movements of the necklace, and equally easy to slow it down as the movement of the necklace gets weaker. When to stop the pulse you decide - just place the necklace in your participants' lap and stop moving your tongue. They won't notice your regular pulse and most of the time they wont even have found your regular pulse to begin with. Their starting point will be your 'tongue pulse'.

"As I started by writing, this looks, feels and sounds like a real hypnotic routine but obviously it's not. It's a very easy way to get your participant and/or audience to believe you can indeed do what you claim to. Imagine the difference it will make going into a "proper" hypnotic routine from here on in? Your credentials have been verified, from here on in it's easy.

"The ball in the armpit is an old trick of the trade. I don't know who invented it, I certainly didn't. The same probably goes for the 'tongue pulse too, I'm sure. Somebody must have thought of this before me so credits to him/her. If I can take credit for anything in this routine I'd like it to be for the toilet paper ball." ☺

15

In Daily Life...

Although staying on the subjects of suggestion and rapport, we hope you'll forgive us for now taking a short detour away from performance magic to look at how you can use what you're learning here just as effectively in your daily life too. Obviously, you can use anchors to create positive emotions within yourself, but you can also create quite life-changing effects very simply with other things we've looked at here too.

Being able to read the signals other people put out is of course only half of the process. It must be obvious by now that if you also know how to control what your own signals say about you then you're in full control of the way you're perceived by others. Just how important that is may not be apparent at first. But when you consider that the outcome of almost every interaction you've ever had with another human being has rested on who they thought you were - and after an assessment that may have only lasted seconds - you realise just how important it really is.

We use Tells to let other people know when we're interested in them, love them, hate them, fear them, feel dominant over them - there are really very few of our deepest thoughts that we don't continually reveal through Tells. And any of us can already, with little or no practise, get people to think that we're sad, angry, mad, or stupid, simply by mimicking the Tells we're all familiar with that denote these emotions.

If you want to totally change your persona in the eyes of others there is no easier way than to simply choose to 'wear' a set of Tells that show you in a positive light. You want to win friends, get a better job, get more opportunities and even get served faster at Burger King? Simple, no tablets or surgery, no course to buy - look happy and confident.

According to various polls and studies over the last 30 years and more, visually happy, confident, well-adjusted people get offered more opportunities, more promotion, get served faster, get more respect and even seem to have better luck than those less well-adjusted amongst us.

Forget looks and clothes to make an impression in the first instance, some of the world's most desirable people have faces like stunned Mullet - but display enough apparent self-confidence and happiness to make them disarmingly attractive to us nonetheless.

And would most of us really know if the signals that any of these people were putting out were not actually real? Probably not. For many people in the public eye, the signals they display for the cameras are far from being a real indication of who they are in their private lives. They're just adept at manipulating and displaying the right Tells. So why shouldn't we be too?

Point 1: We, and the rest of the world, will base our opinion of who you are pretty much solely on what your body language tells us about you.

Now, you might already have realised the above a long time ago and feel we're stating the obvious here. But before you turn the page to look for something more meaningful, we'd like you to consider this and reply honestly - are you really and truly acting upon this 'obvious' piece of information when you need to? Are your Tells and signals saying far more than you realise, or not enough? What do other people really think of you and why? What signals are you actually sending out?

Ian: "I was in intensive care for a while a few years ago. Nothing life-threatening, but what I had made me feel pretty rough for a few weeks after I came out of hospital. Although the symptoms of my illness had lessened, for quite a while I just didn't feel right and I was displaying this very strongly in my body language. I felt fragile, particularly when I was in crowds, so I tended to hunch over and even limped slightly for some reason. What made it worse was that the after-effects of the illness just didn't seem to be going away.

"Then one day I was bumbling along, hugging the walls and mentally shouting, "Sick person coming through!", when I realised that although I didn't feel wonderful I wasn't really that bad at all anymore. So, why the limp? Why the hunch? What was I doing showing this body language to the world? I wasn't sure anymore. It had just become a part of me.

"Feeling slightly embarrassed, I straightened up and relaxed. It felt good to let go of the hunch, so I went for broke and dropped the limp too and took a few practise steps. Despite my trepidation, nothing broke off me and the sky didn't fall down. I suddenly felt a lot better, more confident, even well. In a few minutes I began to feel healthier than I had for months just because I'd dropped not only my 'I'm ill' display face, but lost the feelings that went along with it too."

You'll see similar people every day who frown constantly, have hunched shoulders, squints and limps because they're trying to let people know how they feel - despite some of the causes of these signals occurring tens of years before. But that simple act of displaying how you feel, whether to someone else or just yourself, is very, very powerful, because it creates your mental state. Sustaining a tell, such as a frown, keeps you feeling the emotions that caused it. It's a little like a feedback system. You feel down, you show it as a Tell. But sustaining the Tell keeps you feeling down and makes the depression grow even deeper. You display a stronger Tell in response, etc, etc.

You can cause yourself just as many problems with the Tells you put on in pretence of something as you do with 'real' signals. For example, you might be hoping to take the afternoon off work and are pretending to have a cold or headache. We can guarantee you that after just a very short period of pretence you really will start to feel off-colour or even quite ill, simply by reproducing the signals associated with illness.

Now what's so incredible about this of course is that you are meant to be the one doing the fooling here. You aren't doing this to a subject who has no knowledge of suggestion, you *know* you aren't ill. All you're doing is play-acting with the full knowledge that you aren't really sick at all. But the acting out of the correct posture, expression and voice of an ill person will be based on your previous knowledge of what it's like to be ill. In simply acting out how it feels to be ill you're inflicting some of the actual symptoms of illness upon yourself. You just start to feel a bit off-colour at first, then suggestion does the rest. You create, even in the face of your own knowledge of your actual well-being, a real illness.

This of course has far-reaching repercussions. Think that you're ill and you will become ill. Feel down and you will become down. Pretend you're happy and you will become happy. We become who we portray ourselves to be. Every day we build for ourselves the person we want to appear to be, consciously or subconsciously deciding - and showing to others through various physical signals - that we are happy, sad or indifferent.

To imagine is to create your own reality - who you pretend to be, you become.

But please note that we're not saying, 'Smile and everything will be alright'. What we *are* saying is that acting happy and displaying happy non-verbal signs create a real physical effect that helps engender an increased sense of well-being. How strong that feeling is depends on the state of the person at the time of wearing them. Obviously, if you're in emotional turmoil or deep depression then the feel-good chemicals doing this releases will have a lesser effect than if you're calm and more centred. This isn't a panacea to rid you of worries and depression, but a way of stopping neutral or slightly 'down' feelings turning into something much deeper. Many of us spend much of our lives in a state of not feeling very much at all. Not happy, not sad, but feeling flat and slightly distant from the world. In this kind of state it's common to let neutrality slip towards boredom or depression, when there's just as much opportunity, with methods like the above, to take yourself towards a far happier state.

Neither are we trying to say that hiding your depression or pretending to yourself that it doesn't exist will make it go away. However, you have to understand that the posture and non-verbal signs you display when depressed both deepen and sustain the depression. If you can go against your natural urge to slump your shoulders forward and let your face and eyes sag there's no doubt that it lessens the depth of depression.

We can also, for a variety of reasons, get hooked on displaying depression when it's gone, or can't extricate ourselves from *having* to display it when it's gone because it's expected of us. If we can give ourselves a way out, a more positive feeling to base 'happiness' on rather than try and dig our way out of depression alone, then why not use it?

Signals and Employment?!?

We know - could it be much further from mentalism? But our subconscious awareness of people's signals is of course pronounced enough to affect every aspect of our lives.

Ian: "As an Employment Coach I came across the results of a research poll one day, where employers were asked;

1) When you give a job interview, what will you primarily tend to base your decision to employ or not employ on?

2) How long will it take for you to come to that decision?

"For over 55% of respondents in the USA, the answer to question '1' was - body language. The answer to question '2'? 40 seconds.

"You might object (as many regularly did) that this is unfair, that few people in a job interview are going to be at their confident best. Why then do interviewers base this decision on simple body language at a point of such high stress and why so quickly? What about your skills? Your past experience, eagerness, Gucci shoes and 10 page CV?

"Simply because we all do this same, more or less immediate assessment of everyone we meet. Fair or not it's pretty much all we have to go on until we can really get to know someone. And after all, if you can be calm under pressure you're more than likely the kind of person they're looking for. In these tick-box application form days, an interviewer will in most cases not have the luxury of getting to know you and in fact may not have even read your CV or know anything about the job you're applying for. They *have* to base their decision on what their gut instinct tells them about you, which will tend to be far more accurate than most 'creative' CV's.

We've developed this ability to help us survive, assessing those we meet as quickly as possible to weed out those who may be a threat to us. It doesn't matter that our assessment may be well wide of the mark, one has to be made before we will allow ourselves to interact fully with someone we don't know.

Point 2: It doesn't matter how fair the above is, all you need to understand is that in the eyes of those you meet, happy is good, unhappy is bad.

Luckily, selling yourself as being happy and confident, even when you're not is surprisingly easy. All you have to do is emulate the correct 'confident' signals. But be careful not to take this all too far - this isn't confident with a sneer and a supercilious attitude. This is simply happy and well-adjusted.

To look confident relies on sending out just a small number of signals that others will instinctively recognise. Remember though, this isn't just a case of pretending to be confident and that's that. These elements of correct posture and body language will give you real feelings of confidence through psycho-physical reactions. Who you pretend to be you become.

Ian: "I don't know of any research that's looked at this kind of thing in any detail, but in my experience with meditation that there's no doubt about the power of posture. What happens may be due to the release of endorphins (our bodies own 'feel good' drugs) or something else, but whatever it is, it works. Get the right head and shoulder position and you'll feel more positive, confident, happier and more relaxed within a few seconds."

In the earlier chapters you've already learned to observe and note the other main signals that show tension or relaxation in others, so you can easily at least look relaxed when you need to. To pull off looking confident merely needs a few simple additions:

Head position

Your head position transmits the most important signals of all to others, instantly displaying everything from fear and dominance to your level of fatigue. To put your head in a confident position;

Shoulders relaxed and pulled slightly back, imagine that you're a Flamenco dancer. Hold your head up straight and turn your head towards one shoulder, looking down your nose as though you were watching someone with disdain. You should notice that you get a feeling at the back of your skull as though you're trying to rotate it slightly upwards and forwards over the top of your head. Slowly turn back to face the front. Your chin is now slightly drawn in and your head should feel as though it's being held up by a thread that runs through the centre of your crown.

Relax, don't rush this at all. Try it for a few seconds, relax and try it again, easing yourself into it rather than trying to get it right by forcing yourself into place. Obviously if you're holding this posture very tightly you aren't relaxed and wont be able to feel the difference it will make. Relax.

Spine

Correct head position needs a straight back to complete the illusion. It's obviously no good having a perfectly aligned head but a hunched back, so check your whole posture in a mirror to see how you stand. Although getting the right head position will help your spine alignment, it will help far more if your spine's in the right position before you work on your head.

Hands

Slow hand movements denote openness and calmness. Keeping them away from the centre of your body and no higher than your solar plexus emphasises this. You'll note that when people are agitated they'll tend to have their hands above this height and will keep their hands around their groin or solar plexus to protect them. Open hands, away from the sides of the body denote calm and welcome.

Voice

Slow, steady speech, preferably in lower registers.

16

Operator's Notes

As some of you may already have guessed, both of the experiments in the chapter, 'The Analysis Machine', are complete nonsense, but they're an excellent example of how suggestion can work to create illusory effects in people - even in those who already understand how powerful suggestion can be. But don't worry if you were fooled. As when creating any good suggestion, we gave the effect a provenance, a desirable outcome and, for those of you who did find tangible results, your mind did the rest. Note that in the introduction to the first experiment we described the feelings you might get very broadly and from two ends of the tactile spectrum, 'Does it now feel slicker, more adhesive, or perhaps smoother - or as some users say 'runnier'?' No matter *what* you felt as you did the experiment it will be somewhere between the two. The added phrase, '...or as some say, 'runnier'...' giving the impression not only that other people have tried this, but have successfully found a particular sensation associated with it.

The second experiment is even more fraught with opportunities for self-deception for both subject and performer.

- Even if you don't' explain anything about what you're doing to the subject, they'll expect you to find some difference between the objects, otherwise what's the point of the test?
- How consistent can your downward pressure be on their wrist? Do you really know that you're pushing with the same strength each time?
- Is the subject resisting with the same force every time?
- Are you too expecting there to be a difference?
- Even if you've tried to double blind yourself by getting the subject to pick up an *unknown* object in either experiment, you'll still expect there to be a difference between the two. If one seems hard to press down you might actually subconsciously press a bit

harder/softer the next time to make sure that there is a difference. People will do this test and happily count a complete reversal of the outcome as a success, 'proving' that this works.

- Far more problems can come about if you've told the subject what to expect before you try this, as you're then working with their expectations. With the right kind of patter and motivation to back up the 'science' of this remarkable experiment, many subjects will continually, though unknowingly, create a difference for you.

Though here we're just using this as a bit of fun, the real worry is that these two 'experiments' form the basis of a lot of accepted alternative medical practises, with the second in particular an integral part of many modern therapies, such as Applied Kinesiology. Beware when looking at alternative and complementary medical methods, fortunes have been made by selling the same simple processes we described in 'The Analysis Machine' to both patients and practitioners.

The problem is too that if you were to have read the chapter without this explanation, who knows what it might have prompted you to believe? We have a strange but understandable quirk of nature which makes us tend to believe ardently in the first explanation of things we hear or read about. Books in particular carry an unspoken authority to most people and we find it hard to believe that any book might have got into print without being fully verified somewhere along the line first. But it isn't our faith in the word of authors that's the problem, but our subsequent refusal to later believe alternate explanations, no matter how much proof they might carry.

The book ' The Third Eye' (1956), is a good example of our refusal to let go of 'first in' information. Written by one Tuesday Lobsang Rampa, the author claimed to have been born into a wealthy Tibetan family and to have been a monk, who over many years of tribulations studied - and mastered - Tibetan Buddhism. He then purportedly underwent an operation to open his 'Third Eye', which gave him incredible psychic powers which allowed him to sense realms of existence far beyond our own. With its broad and intriguing tales of life and esoteric practises in a Lhasa monastery, the book sold exceptionally well.

Sadly, eventually it was discovered that the author was in fact one Cyril Henry Hoskins, born in Devon, England, the son of a plumber. When confronted with the truth Hoskins wasn't at all phased, but claimed that although may have been born Cyril Henry Hoskins, his body had been taken over by Rampa's spirit. So, according to him, all the information he had written was true. Rather than this making people think they may have been duped by 'The Third Eye', it gave readers a plausible reason to continue to believe in the story as they'd first imagined it. Despite his unveiling as an impostor and the growing realisation that what he wrote bore very little relationship to the real practises of Tibetan Buddhism, it didn't put off the majority of readers. Though the market for his following titles was smaller, Hopkins went on to write another twelve successful books under the name of Rampa before his death in 1981. There's nothing quite so lasting in our own minds as what we want to believe to be true.

Hopkins story is far from being an isolated case. Crop Circles, channelled spirits, spoon bending and a host of other once supposed mysterious events that galvanised thousands of followers have also been shown to be not quite what they first seemed. The point is that we will always tend to cling tenaciously to what we first believe to be the truth about almost anything, even in the face of absolute proof to the contrary. This is what gives everything from alternate therapies and cults to whacky science and urban myths their power. None of us wants to believe that we've been misled so simply by the assumed authority of the written word, or television, or that man down the street who seems to know a lot about Reiki. First in, last out.

For more experiments like the 'Analysis Machine', take a look at the inspiration for it in a wonderful volume called, 'Mind Machines You Can Build!', by G.Harry Stine. This book is a must read if you'd like to see excellent examples of the clever use of omissions, normalisations and generalisations - and of course, suggestion too.

17

Treat With Caution

Martin: "I don't want to cause anyone any embarrassment with this story, I'm just trying to make a point that will hopefully stop you from falling into one of the many traps that we NLP'ers can create for ourselves. One area for concern is what NLP describes as 'Modelling', the idea that if we mimic another's skills and outward appearance we can somehow be just as adept as they are in a range of professions. A common example in NLP is Modelling a powerful motivational speaker - which is in fact is one of the few abilities that this method *may* help you gain.

"But my point here isn't to ponder how much time and effort people all over the World might be putting into modelling, but to ask how many high-level practitioners don't understand (or at least *seem* not to understand) the limitations of something they've spent such a long time learning? As you'll already know from mentalism, there are all kinds of ways that we can create the appearance of a variety of skills, but it doesn't make them real. If NLP or hypnosis offers the right things, pandering to people's dreams of success, many will readily allow themselves to believe that they are possible.

"Some years ago I got an assignment from an American corporation to set up a Danish branch of their company from scratch. That meant hiring a lot of people and getting them to work together - and fast. I'd used NLP techniques for motivational building for years and I wanted the group of people I had hired to go through a motivational/team-building crash course using these methods. As I wouldn't be able to train the entire workforce myself, I found two renowned external NLP instructors who had an excellent reputation for this line of work. So, I set up a meeting with them, which ended up becoming a dinner invitation for my girlfriend and I.

"We had a pleasant evening and, as expected, the pair spent a lot of time emphasising their credentials and continually tried to gain rapport with both my girlfriend and I; but with no regard for the idea that 'less is more', that we talk about elsewhere in this book. Not a problem, but something I found a bit strange and unnecessary considering their education and background in NLP.

"After dinner I thought I'd try out a few mentalist routines with NLP/Hypnotic elements in them that I was sure my hosts would know and use, but placing them in a different context to see what their reaction would be to them. I thought that they would see what I was doing for what it really was and that we would joke about it and end up having an interesting conversation about how these techniques could be used in areas they might never have thought of before. With tongue in cheek I began by weaving a story about how many of my NLP/Hypnotic skills had evolved into skills which went way beyond the normal usage, and I set about supporting this assertion by doing a couple of basic routines.

"The first thing that really surprised me was the fact that they totally bought into my claim. Instead of laughing and shaking their heads in amusement at the idea that the skills we all shared could be used in ways they had never thought of, they hurriedly started modelling me to figure out how they too could take their skills to this 'level'. I continued doing routines throughout the evening and, instead of seeing them for what they really were, they just seemed genuinely happy, perplexed and intrigued that their 'trade' could actually be taken to such extremes. For all I know they're still at it now, trying to Model the 'Nyrup method' and describing our meeting as a pivotal moment in their lives!☺"

The point is that anyone - even the so called 'powers that be' who should really understand the limitations of what they do - can be tricked into thinking that NLP can do far more than it's really able to. Don't allow yourself to also believe that anything will work just because it's labelled NLP or Hypnosis. There's just as much trickery and self-delusion going on in both of these areas as anywhere else where fortunes are to be made. Whether we're talking about NLP, hypnosis or Pyramid Selling, those who know the real facts about them (but who've paid a lot of money to learn what may not necessarily be based entirely on truth) will do their damnedest to appear to support the methods of what they in turn may go on to sell to others. This may sound like bitter cynicism, but as you may probably have already realised, people lie when it comes to making money. Of course there are things that should remain secret within the realms of magic and mentalism, but shouldn't we at least tell the truth to each other within our own community? What good does it do the novice mentalist to buy expensive books and tricks supposedly based on 'dark and dangerous' NLP that isn't, or daft 'tried and tested' hypnosis methods? Or even have them believe that one single person invented methods of linguistic deception when they've been around ever since we began to develop language? Has it all become more about selling books than passing on knowledge?

As we said right at the beginning of this book, don't take our word or anyone else's for everything that's said about NLP, Hypnosis or any of their astoundingly silly derivatives. Only experience and a firm understanding of what works *for you* - and why - will help you use their real assets without becoming bound up in taking everything they offer at face value.

And Finally

Well, that's it for this book, we hope that you've found enough here to inspire you to try some of the things we suggest to base your effects on. We look forward to seeing you again for our next title. With thank's for your time and patience,

Martin Nyrup & Ian Harling, December 2004.